The Medtronic Murders

How Medtronic, Incorporated put
355,000+ individuals at risk
for sudden cardiac death

A guide for suing Medtronic without
being part of a class action suit

ABOUT THE AUTHOR

Don Alexander is 73 years old and lives with his wife, Elaine, in Rocky Mount, Missouri along the Lake of the Ozarks. Don and Elaine have two adult children, Dr. Blake Daniel Alexander and Jenifer Leigh Alexander (Massart), housewife and mother.

Don earned a triple Bachelor of Science degree and a Doctorate in law (Juris Doctor) attending Missouri University, Washington University, Hannibal-LaGrange University and St. Louis Baptist College as an adult night student between 1960 and 1990. He worked his way from common laborer to salesman, to police officer, to production foreman, to industrial engineer, to senior business analyst, to international business consultant between 1958 and 1974. Don provided consulting services to more than 200 different Corporate Chief Executives between 1974 and 1996. From 1996 to 2005, Don ran his own construction business building and rehabbing residential and commercial properties.

Don retired in 2005 to provide custodial care for his father who died in 2008 at age 95. Don has written twelve books and two screenplays which are all available at Amazon.com (for information on titles and synopsis on each title, go to MedtronicMurders.com and click on website page identified as "Books by Don Alexander"). Just click on the book(s) you wish to preview; or in the books search bar at www.Amazon.com enter title and add "by Don Alexander." Then follow prompts.

Book Chapters

1.   Barring the courthouse doors to the poor and politically unconnected

2.   Bribery, conspiracy, murder and dereliction of duty by prosecutors to indict corporate killers

3.   Federal preemption of state law when medical devices manufacturers are sued for personal injuries

4.   What citizens need to know to act as their own attorney and samples of judicial corruption

5.   A complete guide and required documents to sue Medtronic for damages in your county circuit court

Dedicated to:

All the individuals ripped off, murdered
or injured by Medtronic defibrillators known
to the medical communities to be potentially
defective, extremely dangerous and fatal to
a predictable percentage of heart patients
prior to implantation and wiring of the killer
defibrillator to the hearts of unsuspecting
senior citizens suffering from a deadly heart
arrhythmia and/or potentially fatal heart
fibrillation.

AUTHOR'S FOREWORD

For all those Medtronic victims injured by a Medtronic defibrillator containing a recalled Sprint Fidelis lead or a recalled CHI 4420L battery, it has become possible to sue Medtronic in the Circuit Court of each victim's county of residence.

Any previous settlement agreement with Medtronic pursuant to a class action suit or pursuant to a MDL settlement (such as the one before Judge Kyle in Minnesota) will not bar a state suit filed against Medtronic based upon criminal bribery, criminal conspiracies and criminal consumer fraud for four reasons:

(1)   the prior settlement agreements were based entirely upon product liability legal theories of recovery of damages and NOT upon injuries suffered as the direct result of criminal bribery of physicians, criminal

conspiracies between the party offering the bribe (Medtronic) and the individuals agreeing to accept the bribes (implanting physicians and hospitals acting in complicity with the bribed physicians) in exchange for defrauding heart patients into accepting implantation with a cardiac device known within the medical communities to be potentially defective, extremely dangerous and fatal to a predictable percentage of those implanted with the faulty defibrillators;

(2) the product settlement agreements specifically stated that the settlements pertained to product liability claims under product liability laws applicable to the manufacturer (Medtronic);

(3) the criminal bribery, criminal conspiracies and criminal consumer fraud were not public knowledge until December 12, 2011 when the United States Department of Justice (USDOJ) announced its findings resulting from a multi-year investigation pertaining to Medtronic's bribery of implanting physicians. Therefore, the statute of limitations applicable to state suits filed

against Medtronic for intentional wrongful acts involving multiple criminal conspiracies (with hospital and physician complicity) did not begin to run until December 12, 2011;

and (4) the time window for the relevant statute of limitations is the same time window that applies to the question of "when did Medtronic's victims have any standing to sue Medtronic for intentional injuries inflicted pursuant to criminal bribery, criminal conspiracies and criminal consumer fraud?" The date of the USDOJ announcement is the same date that answers the question "when did Medtronic become chargeable with the criminal acts that damaged the people filing suit in state courts?" This "chargeable date" is well beyond the date of the above described product liability settlement agreements. Such "later criminal acts" by Medtronic are specifically excluded from the product liability settlement agreements.

However, it is best to file the state suits and get the suits officially recorded prior to December 12, 2012 because the "intentional torts (damages caused by criminal acts) statute of limitations" varies from state to state (from one to five years).   An intentional tort simply means an intentional wrongful act that causes personal or financial injuries to another individual.

The state suits must be filed in the appropriate county circuit courts within the intentional torts statute of limitations that applies to each victim's state of residence.

Civil suits against a major corporation are very expensive and either the individual filing suit or the individual's attorney must be willing to invest from several hundred thousand dollars to two and a half million dollars or more to get the case to trial. Seldom, however do such cases get to trial but rather are settled out-of-court.

Few, if any law firms regardless of size and financial resources, will make such an upfront investment in order to represent an individual or a small number of individuals. That is why class actions law suits are the usual choice for suing major corporations that can hire the world's best and most successful lawyers.

The problem with such class action law suits involving thousands of victims is that the lawyers and administrators get most of the money whether in the form of a jury award or an out-of-court settlement.

Moreover, the "Plaintiff's Steering Committee" lawyers do all the legal work in return for several million dollars allocated to each law firm making up the committee from any jury award or settlement fund. The other lawyers rip off the victims to the tune of 30% to 40% of the individual awards for simply getting a victim to join the class action and writing a few letters or making a few phone calls to "keep their clients periodically advised" as to what is happening between the judge, the administrators, the Plaintiffs' Steering Committee, the Defense attorneys, and the corporation being sued.

Lawyers other than those on the steering committee basically do nothing but collect their 30% or more contingency fees for "getting their client(s) signed up."

Consequently, the only way for individuals damaged by a mega-buck corporation to actually recover in proportion to damages suffered is to file an individual suit in state court under state tort laws not subject to federal preemption. A suit brought in federal court will wind up as part of "a multi-district litigation consolidation" which will drag on for years to enrich lawyers and class action administrators.

For example, the Medtronic Sprint Fidelis Multi-district Product Liability Litigation before Judge Kyle in Minnesota dragged on from October 2007 until October 2012. The lawyers and administrators got around 46% of the settlement fund, 40% was held back to reimburse Medicare,

Medicaid and private insurance carriers, and the 15,000 or so victims were allocated the other 14% with the largest individual fund allocation going to the survivors of those killed by Medtronic's defective defibrillators.

This book provides a step-by-step procedure for filing the above described state suits against Medtronic such that a lawyer need not be involved before the case has progressed to the point that interrogatories, depositions, subpoenas, requests for documents, and requests for admissions can be scheduled (this "discovery process" should be handled by an attorney).

Because the facts and circumstances that will apply to each individual suit filed will be the same (except for personal information as to victim, implanting hospital, implanting physician, exact nature of injuries, defibrillator and leads serial number and model number), this book contains the information needed prior to turning the case over to an attorney at the discovery stage of the court proceedings.

Keep in mind that the state suits are not a class action nor a Multi-district litigation forum in a federal court. The cases will be individual suits in counties scattered across the United States.

An attorney contingency fee is a fee that is based entirely upon a percentage of damages awarded to the victim. If no damages are awarded, the attorney has earned no fee.

Don Alexander <u>does not </u>represent any of the individuals who file suit using this book. Rather, he is sharing his personal experiences representing himself.

CHAPTER ONE

Barring the courthouse doors to the poor and politically unconnected

Note: The reader should not be concerned with the language and complexity of the legal pleadings and other documents used in this chapter as examples of the corruption of our legal system. The important thing is to grasp the obvious corruption of the system irrespective of the legal jargon contained in the pleadings and documents. Chapter five will provide a simple step by step format for filing suit in the county "state courts."

As set forth in the United States Constitution and in the constitution of every state, the American legal system is the finest among nations. The American Republic is described as "government by the rule of law" and symbolized by Blindfolded Justice holding forth a balanced scale indicating equal justice for all regardless of financial state, race, color or creed.

Perhaps such a lofty claim was valid at some period in our history but that era disappeared into the total corruption of American jurisprudence manipulated by a legal fraternity that reins from the municipal city courts to the Supreme Court of the United States. While this statement sounds like a wild unsubstantiated claim, this book will set forth in this and following chapters the undeniable proof that our legal system is driven by attorneys and judges who are interested in their own legal careers within a transparent legal fraternity; and who could care less about the actual truth concerning the criminal and civil complaints being ruled upon by political scalawags hidden beneath judicial robes.

Although the corruption involving civil suits is unspeakably disgraceful, the plight of criminal defendants is even worse. The US Constitution firmly provides for appointment by presiding judges of legal counsel for indigent criminal defendants. But, who gets appointed? The least experienced, most bumbling attorneys who are either fresh out of law school or too inept to cut the mustard in private practice can usually get appointed to defend indigent criminal defendants. Law school graduates often take a job with a public defender's office rather than serve as a gopher for ten years or so in a large, politically connected law firm while trying to work their way to the "senior associate level."

The public defenders appointed to defend the vast majority of criminal defendants are usually opposed by seasoned prosecutors who use every dirty trick ever imagined to get a guilty verdict regardless of the guilt or innocence of the individual on trial for his/her freedom and/or very life. The presiding judges know precisely what is going on but will invariably favor the prosecutor over the public defender because prosecutors generally move on to political offices that can hinder or further the judge's political career. Even federal judges appointed for life would like to move up to the US Court of Appeals and then hopefully have a shot at a Presidential appointment to the US Supreme Court bench. The US Supreme Court hopefuls must be willing to bow humbly to political supporters for a chance to convert their personal opinions and biases into "the law of the land."

The overwhelming majority of American citizens know virtually nothing about the complex questions of law which are constantly argued before the appellate courts and the US Supreme Court. For more than half a century the politically connected who wrangle an appointment to the US Supreme Court do not confirm and apply the existing law. Rather, they legislate their opinions and biases into law under the transparent pretense of interpreting what the "founding fathers" **_really_** intended when drafting the US Constitution (which can easily be read correctly by a fifth grader). What is difficult to understand about the US Constitutional guarantee that the right of citizens to bear arms shall not be infringed.

The politicians who want to push the United States into a global government, run by a benevolent dictator, want to collect our guns so that we cannot defend ourselves against government tyranny. Guns, they opine, kill people. Well, so do hammers, ice picks, knives, axes, hatchets, choke devices, human hands, bricks and stones, etc., etc. Shall we cut off every one's hands so that no human dies from being choked? Nevertheless, we elect these demagogues to rule over us. This same apathy is the reason our legal system has become totally corrupted.

The vulgarly overpaid executives running our major corporations (like Medtronic, Incorporated) take advantage of our greedy lawyers and dishonest judges to ripoff the public treasury and to pay out millions in law suit settlements and massive bribes in order to pass billions through to bottom line profits by dumping defective inventories into the stream of interstate commerce. Hundreds of millions are regularly paid out in bribes to government regulatory officials, to politicians, to law enforcement officers, and to health care providers.

An outstanding example of judicial abuse in

progress is the August 27, 2012 ruling by Federal Judge Nannette Laughrey denying the following motion for her recusal as presiding judge in a civil action against Medtronic:

IN THE UNITED STATES DISTRICT COURT
FOR THE WESTERN DISTRICT OF MISSOURI
CENTRAL DIVISION

)   CASE # 2:12-cv-04104-NKL

DONALD K. ALEXANDER,)

Plaintiff,   )   **Jury Trial Requested**

VS.   )

MEDTRONIC, INC., AND   )

CH ALLIED SERVICES, INC.)

(DBA AS BOONE   )

HOSPITAL CENTER)   )

Defendants.   )

**PLAINTIFF ALEXANDER'S MOTION FOR
RECUSAL OF JUDGE NANETTE LAUGHREY AS
FEDERAL DISTRICT JUDGE PRESIDING**

OVER THIS CAUSE OF ACTION

Comes now Plaintiff Pro Se Donald K. Alexander (hereinafter "Alexander") and submits to the Court and opposing counsel Alexander's motion for recusal of Judge Nanette Laughrey for cause as more fully set forth herein.

1.   Two sections of Title 28 of the United States Code *(the Judicial Code) provide standards for judicial disqualification or recusal. Section 455, captioned "Disqualification of justice, judge, or magistrate judge," provides that a federal judge "shall disqualify himself in any proceeding in which his* impartiality *might reasonably be questioned." The same section also provides that a judge is disqualified "where he has a personal bias or prejudice concerning a party, or personal knowledge of disputed evidentiary facts concerning the proceeding"; when the judge has previously served as a lawyer or witness concerning the same case or has expressed an opinion concerning its outcome; or when the judge or a member of his or her immediate family has a financial interest in the outcome of the proceeding. 28 U.S.C. sec. 144, captioned "Bias or prejudice of judge," provides that under circumstances, when a party to a case in a* <u>United States District Cour</u>*t files a "timely and sufficient* <u>Motion</u> *that the judge before whom the matter is pending has a personal bias or prejudice either against him or in favor of an adverse party," the case shall be transferred to another judge.*

    2.   Federal District Judge Nanette Laughrey has a personal history involving Alexander spanning more than twenty years as detailed below and has violated her oath upon admission to the Missouri Bar by refusing to report criminal professional misconduct on the part of David Macoubrie, President of the Missouri State Board of Law Examiners who issued criminal threats to the 1990 Missouri School of Law-Columbia faculty which included Nanette Laughrey. The nature of Mcoubrie's said threats constituted felonious interference with counsel plus a civil rights conspiracy under color of law

to keep Alexander from sitting for the Missouri Bar exam in which said law school faculty acquiesced including Nanette Laughrey. The law school faculty had a fiduciary duty being bound by their personal oaths to report Mcoubrie's said threats to the Missouri Bar Disciplinary Committee.

3.   Although Alexander has been willing for twenty years to forgive the lawyers and judges [including Federal Judges sitting in Kansas City, St. Louis, St. Joseph and Jefferson City plus the 1990 Missouri Supreme Court bench) who all either initially or subsequently became entangled with said civil rights conspiracy under color of law (which carries up to ten years in a federal prison)], Defendant Medtronic's lawyers in this case before the Court have unburied the accusations levied against Alexander during the course of said civil rights conspiracy under color of law in an attempt (which apparently worked) to influence Judge Laughrey's rulings in this case before the federal bench.

4.   Whether Judge Laughrey was amenable to such shysterism by Medtronic's lawyers is not a

deciding factor pertaining to her recusal under *Title 28 U.S.C. Sections 455 and 144 and further commented on in Liteky v. United States, U.S. Supreme Court (1994).* The facts and circumstances alleged by Alexander follow below and justify both Judge Laughrey's recusal and a change of venue to the Federal District Court sitting in Springfield, Missouri which is the only Division within the Western District of Missouri wherein judical bias and maliciousness has not yet been demonstrated toward Alexander.

5.   Who exactly is Judge Laughrey as pertains to Alexander? Well folks, we have to go back to 1990 or so when Nanette Laughrey was teaching the Federal Rules of Civil Procedure at Missouri University School of Law –Columbia Campus where Alexander was scheduled to graduate with a Juris Doctor degree. Alexander was involved in a major breach of contract suit against an association of manufactures who were robbing Alexander of approximately 5.5 million dollars in incentive earnings. The association was represented

by Evans & Dixon Law Firm. Geree Langton was at the time Senior Appeals Partner for Evans & Dixon and also a sitting member of the Missouri State Board of Law Examiners. Henry Menghini was a senior partner at Evans & Dixon. Jim Devine was teaching professional ethics and constitutional law at MU School of Law, Tim Heinsz was Dean of MU School of Law, Betty Wilson and Loramel Shurtleff were sitting members of the 13th Judicial Circuit Bar Committee. David Macoubrie was president of the Missouri State Board of Law Examiners. (Now, folks, this is where the rubber meets the road. This is a typical example of how the political scalawags and legal scum administer our legal system). The legal profession is self-policing. All members of the Missouri Bar swore an oath to report any instance of professional misconduct on the part of any other Bar member or any practicing lawyer regardless of Bar affiliation. All Bar members are considered "Officers of the Court" and presumed to be oozing integrity, honesty and untainted professionalism.

  6. Being a pro se litigant, Evans and Dixon's

senior partners did not take Alexander seriously and assigned a novice firm attorney to oppose Alexander. She rather quickly failed to comply with the Missouri Rules of Civil Procedure and was faced with a imminent default judgment. Evans & Dixon called in some IOU's to permit backdating some critical responsive pleadings and filed a false affidavit in the court file. Alexander, along with Judge Kenneth Romines discovered the backdating and false affidavit whereupon Alexander filed professional misconduct charges with the Missouri Bar against Henry Menghini who orchestrated the back dating and false affidavit. Henry Menghini called Alexander at home and reminded Alexander that he was graduating from law school but must sit for the bar exam and it would be up to Evans & Dixon as to whether Alexander would be allowed to sit for the exam. Mr. Menghini further warned Alexander that he must be willing to trade favors with other bar members. Alexander, believing life too short and eternity too long to associate with such human trash, more or less told

Menghini to get lost and that his threat would also be reported to the Missouri Bar Disciplinary Committee.

7.   The association would have been bankrupted by paying Alexander his earned incentives such that Alexander did not try to squeeze blood out of a turnip. As the date drew nearer for the bar exam Alexander was summoned for a brutal oral exam before the 13th Judicial Circuit Bar Committee upon which sat Betty Wilson and Loramel Shurtleff. The Bar Committee had hired a private detective to find something in Alexander's background that could be used to deny him permission to sit for the bar exam. Having failed in that strategy, the committee wanted to terrorize Alexander and make "a good little lawyer" out of him that would not cause Bar members involved with dishonest activities any disciplinary concerns. Alexander was not intimidated and the Bar Committee recommended that Alexander be seated for the Missouri Bar Exam. However, Geree Langton and her fellow members of the Missouri State Board of Law Examiners were determined to keep Alexander out of the Missouri Bar by denying him

permission to sit for the exam. Alexander received a denial letter from the law board members who explained that Alexander was unfit to sit for the bar exam (pay careful attention, folks) because he resorted to the courts instead of self-help (the board called this "being overly litigious"); because he had been divorced twice; because he had filed bankruptcy in connection with a divorce and bad business venture; and because he had received several traffic tickets as a teenager. (Wow, folks! Did you get that? How much more unfit could a 51 year old law school graduate be???)

8.   Alexander, smelling a civil rights conspiracy initiated by the Missouri State Board of Law Examiners in retribution against him for filing professional misconduct charges against a sitting member's law firm, filed a civil rights conspiracy suit in Federal court. That is when the proverbial shit hit the fan. Not a single member of the Missouri Bar Association would consider representing Alexander but David McCoubrie, President of the Missouri State Board of Law Examiners, believed

that some law professors might be helping Alexander draft his pleadings. So, Mr. McCoubrie issued specific threats to the law school faculty that anyone helping Alexander would feel the wrath of the Missouri Bar (felonious interference with right to counsel). The threat was common knowledge among the law school faculty. James Devine (now deceased) was especially upset as professor teaching professional ethics and constitutional law. He advised Alexander of the threat but said he had boys becoming college age and could not risk his career to report such flagrant professional misconduct. Other faculty members (some, like Nanette Laughrey, hoping for appointment to the bench) likewise refused to report McCoubrie's said misconduct. Alexander was officially denied permission to set for the Missouri Bar Exam.

9.   Alexander taped a conversation with Jim Devine wherein Mr. Devine admitted said threat by McCoubrie. Alexander turned the tape over to Timothy Heinsz, Dean of the Law School. Heinsz was sympathetic but chose not to report McCoubrie. The Federal court in Kansas City (Judge Scott Wright)

branded Alexander's case as frivolous and fined him $10,000 to discourage Alexander from filing an appeal. Alexander's appeals to the Eighth Circuit were tossed out and the US Supreme Court refused to hear Alexander's complaint. Thus, Alexander was effectively barred from the courts without ever setting a foot inside a courtroom to present his complaint and supporting evidence (the taped confession). Because the civil rights conspiracy against Alexander under color of law continued unabated, Alexander filed a second complaint which was also summarily dismissed without a court hearing of any kind. Alexander's second appeal to the Eighth Circuit was dismissed. Alexander then filed a petition for rehearing before the Eighth Circuit and included a "tongue-in-cheek" self-defense using "deadly force argument" to shock the Eight Circuit bench into taking a closer look at what was going down. The Circuit disregarded the petition for rehearing. The Missouri School of Law-Columbia Campus is located in Boone County. Betty Wilson and Loramel Shurtleff egged on by a new assistant Boone County prosecutor filed criminal charges against Alexander for harassment under a Missouri Statute prohibiting hate mail and/or threatening phone calls to a private citizen's residence. Alexander had not placed any phone calls or mailed any hate mail to anyone. Alexander's legal pleading filed with the Eighth Circuit is absolutely privileged with respect to civil or criminal liability but the court can sanction litigants if the court considers the pleading overly offensive.

      10.   The Eighth Circuit did not sanction Alexander or even comment on the pleading. Nevertheless, the Boone County Assistant Prosecutor and a newly appointed circuit court judge railroaded Alexander into a jury trial for harassment where the only jury issue was whether Loramel Shurtleff and Betty Wilson (two sitting members of the 13th Judicial Circuit Bar Committee who hired the private detective to find something "just awful" in Alexander's background) were offended by reading the pleading Alexander filed with the Eighth Circuit. Alexander was convicted of

harassment and spent 90 days in a maximum security prison. Hurray!! for the red, white and blue. (Routine justice in action, folks).

11.   While in prison, Alexander filed a writ of habeas corpus to be released from prison on the grounds that the crime for which Alexander was convicted does not exist in American jurisprudence because all legal pleadings filed with a court of law are absolutely privileged from either criminal or civil liability. Nonetheless, Alexander's said writ was summarily denied and Alexander was forced to serve his entire sentence plus probation. All of the foregoing happened to Alexander because Nanette Laughrey and other law school faculty, in order to remain popular and accepted within the Missouri Bar, refused to come to Alexander's aid and report the direct threats by David Mcoubrie issued to the laws school faculty members. Nanette Laughrey got her appointment to the bench. Hurray for you!!! Nanette.   However, Federal Judge Nanette Laughrey still apparently remembers how she ran up the

back stairs at Missouri School of Law like a ruptured pelican when Alexander asked why Macoubrie's threat was not being reported by the law school faculty members as required by their solemn oath upon admission to the Missouri Bar. As she waddled out of sight, Alexander could hear sweet, integrity oozing, self-policing, paragon of virtue, officer of the court, defender of the legal rights of law students, Professor Nanette Laughrey saying: "I can't get involved with you!!"

WHEREFORE, for the reasons detailed herein, Alexander prays this Court for recusal of Judge Nanette Laughrey as presiding judge in this cause of action as required under Title 28 U.S.C. Sections 455 and 144.

Respectfully submitted,

Donald K. Alexander

Donald K. Alexander

Plaintiff Pro Se

31057 Oak Ridge Drive

Rocky Mount, Missouri 65072

(573) 557-2071

donalexander557@gmail.com

CERTIFICATE OF SERVICE

The undersigned hereby certifies that on the 11th day of June, 2012 a copy of the foregoing Motion For Recusal of Judge Nanette Laughrey filed by Plaintiff Alexander was forwarded by First Class US Mail with postage prepaid to Jonathan H. Garside, Attorney for Defendant CH Allied Services, Inc., at Fox Galvin Law Firm, One South Memorial Drive, 12th Floor, St. Louis, Missouri 63102: and to Patrick Lysaught, attorney for Defendant Medtronic, Incorporated at Baker Sterchi Cowden & Rice, L.L.C. (Law Firm), 2400 Pershing Road, Suite 500, Kansas City, Missouri 64108.

Donald K. Alexander, Plaintiff Pro Se

ADDITIONAL CERTIFICATE OF SERVICE

The undersigned further hereby certifies that service of the foregoing document was made by means of the Notice of Electronic Filing this 11th day of June, 2012, to the following counsel of record by forwarding of said document to the Clerk of the Court for scanning and electronic notice; and further that said document was emailed on June 11, 2012 to opposing counsel at these email addresses:

Jonathan H. Garside

jgarside@foxgalvin.com, dlouis@foxgalvin.com

Patrick Lysaught   lysaught@bscr-law.com, singleton@bscr-law.com

Donald K. Alexander, Plaintiff Pro Se

Federal Judge Richard Kyle (whose son is an attorney and shareholder in a law firm which has openly represented Medtronic) decided that it is okay for Medtronic to dump defective defibrillators into the stream of interstate commerce because, by golly, the FDA is doing such a superb job of overseeing medical device manufacturers and therefore all state law suits against Medtronic are preempted by Federal oversight. Medtronic, fearful of Judge Kyle being overturned on appeal, set up a global settlement fund based upon fraud and misrepresentation as set forth in the following appeal still pending before the US Court of Appeals for the Eighth Judicial Circuit:

CASE NUMBER: **12-1298**

IN THE UNITED STATES COURT OF APPEALS

FOR THE EIGHTH JUDICIAL CIRCUIT

DONALD K. ALEXANDER,

APPELLANT/PLAINTIFF,

V.

WILLIAM A. HAWKINS, SUSAN ALPERT, KATHLEEN ERICKSON DiGIORNO, STEPHEN N. OESTERLE, M.D., GARY ELLIS, AND MEDTRONIC, INCORPORATED, APPELLEES/DEFENDANTS.

ON APPEAL FROM THE U.S. DISTRICT COURT FOR

THE DISTRICT OF MINNESOTA ; AND THE U.S. DISTRICT

COURT FOR THE THE WESTERN DISTRICT OF MISSOURI

CENTRAL DIVISION

MN District Court case # 0:10-cv-03373-RHK-JSM

MO District Court case number 2:10 CV 04081 NKL

APPELLANT/PLAINTIFF'S REPLY BRIEF

To Brief filed by Medtronic Defendants (by Attorney

Daniel L. Ring)

DONALD K. ALEXANDER

31057 OAK RIDGE DRIVE

ROCKY MOUNT, MISSOURI 65072

(573) 557-2071 donalexander557@gmail.com

TABLE OF CONTENTS

APPELLANT/PLAINTIFF'S REPLY TO BRIEF SUBMITTED BY MEDTRONIC DEFENDANTS (THROUGH ATTORNEY DANIEL L. RING)

Appellant/Plaintiff has already replied to brief

submitted by Defendant CH Allied Services Inc. (dba

Boone Hospital Center) and its employees named as co-

Defendants through opposing counsel Jonathan Garside.

Appellant/Plaintiff rests upon his reply already filed in

this consolidated appeal but feels compelled to briefly

reply to the brief submitted by the Medtronic Defendants through opposing counsel Daniel L. Ring (hereinafter "Mr. Ring").

Mr. Ring apparently remembers the proverb
tossed around about 20 years ago in law school: "If the
law and facts are against you, dazzle them with your
bullshit." So, Mr. Ring repeats the same refrain in
multiple recitations while dancing around the extremely
simple issues in this appeal. Moreover, several times Mr.
Ring insinuates that a legal argument cannot be
summarized in a simple statement but must run on and
on like a child begging for a cookie. Then, he has the
unmitigated gall to misrepresent the refusal of the MDL
court clerk to docket the FRCP Rule 60 motion which
prompted Appellant/ Plaintiff to refile the motion in the

transferor Court. He alleges a bald faced lie while hoping that the Circuit Judges don't notice the obvious falsehood he mouths concerning the factual statement alluded to by Appellant/Plaintiff that the MDL clerk did not docket the appeal until after Judge Laughrey referred the motion back to Judge Kyle.

Mr. Ring runs on and on about the multiple filings by Appellant/Plaintiff made necessary by the gross judicial errors inherent in burying Appellant/Plaintiff's Civil RICO suit beneath stalled product liability litigation in order to protect Medtronic from facing a jury to answer for ten years of criminal behavior that killed numerous individuals and injured thousands. Appellant/Plaintiff does not believe that federal Judges are that incompetent. However, the question remains as to why the Civil RICO suit was sent to Judge Kyle initially and why Judge Kyle repeatedly refused to remand the Civil RICO suit for lack of subject matter jurisdiction. Mr. Ring bluffs the Circuit bench by circling Medtronic's wagons crying about how this poor dumb old man just kept filing suit like a legal moron.

Then, Mr. Ring cries crocodile tears about Appellant opting into a settlement agreement and then exhibiting the stupidity to try and opt out via a FRCP Rule 60B motion when Medtronic and Plaintiffs' lawyers were sacrificing so much to be honest and fair with Medtronic's victims. Nothing could be a bigger lie. The settlement agreement was carefully crafted to allow Plaintiffs' lawyers to pocket a hundred million while at the same time protecting Medtronic from being sued by insurance entities like Medicare and Medicaid for the hundreds of millions Medtronic has stolen by filing false

claims, bribing FDA and physicians, and overcharging

the insurers to recover Medtronic bribe money.

Mr. Ring can run on at the mouth until doomsday

and never convince a mongoloid idiot that leading

claimants on to expect an average payout of $33,000

and then whittling that down to one thirty-third of the

expected payout can be justified by any logic, lies, or

otherwise. Oh my, my, Mr. Ring opines. Don't you know

there were a few more claimants that just leaped out of

the woodwork at the last second and caused the average

payout to be slightly reduced. Golly, gee, Medtronic was

laboring in the dark about who its victims are and just

couldn't figure it out until everybody dismissed their

case to recover $33,000 in damages (when most

claimant's damages actually exceeded $80,000; most of

which was money stolen by Medtronic and scheduled to

be reimbursed to those insurers ripped off by

Medtronic). Yes indeed! Medtronic's lawyers and bean

counters just had no clue that Plaintiff's lawyers by the

terms of the settlement scam were going to get a

hundred million and Medicare/Medicaid another

hundred million, administrators and court appointed lead

attorneys five to six million and the 14,000-15,000

Medtronic victims were going to be handsomely

enriched by a whopping average payout of less than one

eightieth of their actual average damages. What a deal!!!

Who in hell would object to the slight reduction from

$33,000 to $1,000 or less.

Mr. Ring also dances around the fact that the

settlement agreement did not represent any more than

smoke and mirrors that was promoted and acclaimed by

Plaintiffs' attorneys as a great deal and pure generosity

on the part of Medtronic since if claimants did not opt

into such a wonderful sacrifice by Medtronic they would

get nothing because of the federal preemption defense.

Claimants were never advised of other legal theories of

recovery of damages to which preemption does not

apply.

Appellant/Plaintiff in opting into the settlement

was trying to obtain funds to have his killer Medtronic

defibrillator surgically removed because researchers

were reporting that the fourth year after implantation

was the most dangerous time and Appellant/ Plaintiff

was entering the fourth year since his implantation and

already had been hospitalized three times in connection

with inappropriate multiple shocking episodes ---- 21

shocks). Plaintiffs' Steering Committee lawyers led Appellant/Plaintiff to believe that he would be allocated as much as $75,000 and would have the money probably in July 2011. In March 2102, Appellant/Plaintiff was allocated $500 dollars. WOW!!! What a deal!! Just a minor decrease in allocation due to a minor underestimation of claimants by a mere 42 percent after the settlement fund had been reduced by roughly 20%. No sir!! No scam going on here. Just a slight calculation error by Medtronic's bean counters due to those precise records kept by Medtronic so that anyone looking at the files just might not notice that every single defibrillator recipient is carefully identified, tracked and kept in the dark as to the Medtronic foreknowledge that their implant might injure or kill them without warning.

Yes! Isn't is really a demonstration of

Medtronic's tender care of it's cardiac implant recipients

that Medtronic had to suffer through billions in profits

from defective and deadly defibrillators and had to pay

out millions to victims injured and survivors of the

folks who succumbed to their defective cardiac

implants. Who in their right mind would think that

reaping ten billion or so in profits and paying out less

than one billion including FDA and physician bribes and

global settlement funding was not a great sacrifice to

compensate people knowingly, intentionally and

recklessly injured or killed by defibrillators known to

Medtronic to be defective, extremely dangerous and

perhaps fatal? Who is this old fart that keeps running

around filing suit to recover medical expenses after we

buried him beneath unrelated product liability litigation

and kicked him around by dazzling Judges with our

brilliance and professional integrity. Doesn't he know

that we "officers of the court" squat over golden toilets

and help put Judges on the bench so that they owe us big

time? What's he doing here taking up the Circuit's

valuable time by claiming that he got scammed by

getting $500 instead of the $33,000 to $75,000 we

bounced between smoke and mirrors?

This old goat is so legally stupid that he thinks

product liability litigation and Civil RICO suits are not

based on the same legal theories of recovery. Moreover,

he don't seem to understand that more than one court

can have jurisdiction over him at the same time. Hell

yes, Grandpa!!! It's done all the time and the nine wise

ones in Washington don't tell us what to do. They said

we can't allow an MDL Court to bootstrap jurisdiction

after being divested of all jurisdiction upon remand to

the transferor Court. We don't find any fault with two

courts having subject matter jurisdiction at the same

time unless it is our client that's getting kicked around.

Finally, Mr. Ring argues that Appellant/Plaintiff's

arguments are without merit and he therefore does not

have to address the diverse legal theories pertaining to

Civil RICO versus product liability or the legal basis for

two courts having subject matter jurisdiction

simultaneously; or how $500 is a minor deviation from

$33,000. Just to make his point more vividly, he cites a

ream of cases that are as different from this case on

appeal as jackrabbits versus kangaroos.

Respectfully submitted,

//Donald K. Alexander, Appellant/Plaintiff

Donald K. Alexander

31057 Oak Ridge Drive
Rocky Mount, Missouri 65072
(573) 557-2071 donalexander557@gmail.com

CERTIFICATE OF COMPLIANCE

The undersigned Appellant/Plaintiff, Donald K. Alexander, certifies that this reply brief complies with FRAP Rule 28 and all sections thereof in that the brief contains   6,853 words and 142 lines in proportionally faced face using 14 point font.

Signature: //Donald K. Alexander,

Appellant /Plaintiff

With respect to the super duper oversight by the FDA and its regulatory functions, the following letter from nine FDA scientists to President Obama is an eye opener (although nothing has really changed):

DEPARTMENT OF HEALTH
AND HUMAN SERVICES

Food and Drug Administration
Office of Device Evaluation
9200 Corporate Boulevard
Rockville, MD 20850

April 2, 2009

The Honorable Barack H. Obama
President of the United States
1600 Pennsylvania Avenue NW
Washington, DC 20500

Dear Mr. President:

The purpose of this letter is to draw your attention to the
frustration and outrage that FDA physicians and
scientists, public advocacy groups, the press, and the
American people, have repeatedly expressed over the
misdeeds of FDA officials. Recent press reports
revealed extensive evidence of serious wrongdoing by
Dr. Andrew von Eschenbach, Dr. Frank M. Torti, top
FDA attorneys, Center and Office Directors, and many
others in prominent positions of authority at FDA. As a
result, Dr. Frank M. Torti, Acting Commissioner and the
FDA's first Chief Scientist, abruptly left the Agency.
But, the many other FDA managers who have failed to
protect the American public, who have violated laws,
rules, and regulations, who have suppressed or altered
scientific or technological findings and conclusions,
who have abused their power and authority, and who
have engaged in illegal retaliation against those who
speak out, have not been held accountable and remain in
place.

On Monday, March 30, 2009, Dr. Joshua Sharfstein,
newly appointed Principal Deputy Commissioner,
assumed the position of Acting Commissioner until Dr.

Margaret Hamburg is confirmed. Numerous FDA
physicians and scientists are certain that Dr. Hamburg
and Dr. Sharfstein will bring the necessary change to
FDA to guarantee integrity, accountability, and
transparency, to ensure that all future decisions are
solely based on science and in accordance with
the laws, rules, and regulations. However, sweeping
measures are needed to end the systemic corruption and
wrongdoing that permeates all levels of FDA and has
plagued the Agency far too long.

The latest example of wrongdoing was reported on
March 23, 2009 from a Federal District Court
Judge who ruled that FDA's decision on the Plan B drug
was "arbitrary and capricious because they were not the
result of reasoned and good faith agency decision-
making." FDA's top leaders at the Center for Drug
Evaluation and Research (CDER) testified that they
"didn't have a choice, and . . . [weren't] sure that [they]
would be allowed to remain [in their positions if they]
didn't agree" to ignore the science and the law. To the
contrary, they should be removed from their positions of
authority precisely because they didn't follow the
science and the law. The judge further ruled that there
was "unrebutted evidence that the FDA's [decision]
stemmed from political pressure rather than permissible
health and safety concerns." The "improper political
influence" and the

many "departures from its own policies" reveal that such FDA officials are incapable of ensuring integrity and science at FDA.

On October 14, 2008, FDA physicians and scientists wrote to members of the House Energy and Commerce Committee reporting that top FDA officials at the Center for Devices and Radiological Health (CDRH) had distorted the scientific review of medical devices and then retaliated against those who brought this to light.

Congressman John Dingell (then Chairman) and Congressman Bart Stupak (Chairman, Subcommittee on Oversight and Investigations) wrote to then FDA Commissioner Dr. Andrew C. von Eschenbach (since resigned), stating that there were "well documented allegations that senior managers within CDRH" had "acted in violation of the law ... [and that] sweeping measures may be necessary to address the distortion of science alleged by so many CDRH scientists."

On January 7, 2009, FDA physicians and scientists wrote to Mr. John Podesta:

"Through this letter and your action, we hope that future FDA employees will not experience the same frustration and anxiety that we have experienced for more than a year at the hands of FDA managers because we are committed to public integrity and were willing to speak out. Currently, there is an atmosphere at FDA in which the honest employee fears the dishonest employee, and not the other way around. Disturbingly, the atmosphere does not yet exist at FDA where honest employees committed to integrity and the FDA mission can act without fear of reprisal. ... America urgently needs change at FDA because FDA is fundamentally broken, failing to fulfill its mission, and because reestablishing a proper and effectively functioning FDA is vital to the physical and economic health of the nation."

On January 13, 2009, the NY Times reported that FDA officials allowed "improper political influence" to guide official FDA actions. The Director of the Office of Device Evaluation, Dr. Donna-Bea Tillman, approved a medical device used for the detection of breast cancer despite the fact that all of the FDA experts involved recommended against approval of the device three times. Dr. Tillman's decision to overrule the FDA experts "followed a phone call from a Connecticut congressman [Christopher Shays]."

On January 26, 2009, FDA physicians and scientists wrote to you directly seeking your help and recommending that "you remove and hold accountable all managers who have ordered, participated in, fostered or tolerated the well-documented corruption, wrongdoing and retaliation at the Agency." That letter was prompted by concerns that FDA officials were planning to investigate physicians and scientists in

retaliation for the January 13, 2009 story in the NY
Times. These concerns were well founded.
On March 13, 2009, one week after another episode
detailing wrongdoing and improper political
influence involving top FDA officials was published in
the Wall Street Journal, Acting Commissioner Dr. Frank
M. Torti and FDA attorneys sprung into action. Their
solution— send an FDA-wide email admonishing FDA
employees that they "must comply with … obligations
to keep certain information … confidential …
[including] e-mail to and from employees within FDA
[that document the] deliberative process" and
threatening that "violation … can result in disciplinary
sanctions and/or individual criminal liability."

Page 3 of 6, Letter to President Obama

These threats did not escape the scrutiny of Senator
Chuck Grassley, Ranking Member of the U.S. Senate
Committee on Finance. In a letter to Dr. Torti on March
24, 2009, Senator Grassley wrote: "Your
memorandum … appears to run contrary to many
statutes protecting executive branch communications
with members of Congress. … I am concerned with the
timing of your memorandum, given some recent high
profile matters concerning your Agency and the release
of information that has shown failures in FDA's
regulatory mission. [This] could be viewed … as an
effort to chill and/or prevent FDA employees from
exercising their rights under whistleblower protection
laws. … Whistleblowers are some of the most patriotic

people I know—men and women who labor, often
anonymously, to let Congress and the American people
know when the Government isn't working so we can fix
it."

The Wall Street Journal and FDA documents
revealed efforts by top FDA officials (including Dr.
von Eschenbach, Dr. Torti, Mr. William McConagha,
and other FDA attorneys) to cover-up their attempts to
improperly influence, obstruct, impede and distort the
due and proper administration of the FDA scientific
regulatory process involving a knee implant device.
According to the Columbia University Journalism
Review, "the [Wall Street] Journal describes a process
in this case that's, well, corrupt. I don't know what else
you'd call it. It even has a smoking gun."

An advisory committee of outside experts, convened to
provide advice on the safety and effectiveness of the
knee implant, was misled and manipulated by Dr. Daniel
Schultz (Director of CDRH) as well as top FDA
attorneys. Dr. Schultz was accused of "stacking the
committee to get the decision the company wanted," and
of falsely stating in an official document that the
conclusions reached by the advisory
committee were "clear" and "unanimous"—to the
contrary, they were not. A letter from Senator Grassley
to Dr. Torti dated March 6, 2009 indicated that Dr.
Schultz and top FDA attorneys had concealed the fact
that two of the authors of a major publication presented

to the advisory committee in support of the knee implant device, had affiliations with the device manufacturer ("the first author of the article is [the manufacturer's] Vice President of Scientific Affairs," Senator Grassley noted).

Dr. Jay Mabrey, Chief of orthopedic surgery at Baylor University Medical Center in Dallas and Chairman of the advisory committee, should be commended for his integrity and willingness to speak out once he became aware of what had transpired. Dr. Larry Kessler, former Director of the Office of Science and Engineering Laboratories at FDA, who had direct knowledge of the advisory committee meeting and process, characterized the process as "show[ing] the FDA at its worst."

The culture of wrongdoing and cover-up is nothing new but is part of a longstanding pattern of behavior. For example, in July 2005, Dr. Daniel Schultz "approved a medical device against the unanimous opinion of his scientific staff," overruling "more than twenty FDA scientists, medical officers and management staff."

  According to the New York Times the decision represented the first time in the agency's history that a director "approved a device in the face of unanimous opposition from staff scientists and administrators beneath him." As described in a Senate Finance Committee report following an investigation led by Senator Grassley, Dr. Schultz never revealed to the public that the FDA scientists, medical officers, and all other staff involved, completely disagreed with his decision. The report also stated that "what remains the same in FDA's approval of a device or a drug is the requirement that data supporting a sponsor's application for approval be scientifically sound. Otherwise health care providers and insurers as well as patients may question the integrity and reliability of the FDA's assessment of the safety and effectiveness of an approved product."– We completely agree.

Page 4 of 6, Letter to President Obama

Amazingly, just 3 weeks ago, on March 6, 2009, it was reported by the consumer advocacy organization Public Citizen that Dr. Tillman "approved a [medical] device that has failed to demonstrate any clinical benefit" and that showed "trends toward higher risks of death."

 According to Public Citizen: The March 6, 2009 approval by Dr. Tillman "bears an eerie resemblance to another device, Intergel, an anti-scarring device intended for pelvic surgeries that also demonstrated reduced scarring without clinically validated outcomes. … Less than two years after Intergel was approved [by Dr. Schultz] the company removed the product from the market due to reports of post-operative pain, foreign body reactions and tissue scarring requiring repeat surgery, including three deaths among women who received it. This history should have given the FDA pause before once again approving a similar device with a questionable safety record."

But now, things may finally change at FDA and meeting
the expectations of the public may become a reality. On
March 14, 2009, an FDA-wide e-mail was sent from the
Acting Secretary of HHS: "Dr. Margaret "Peggy"
Hamburg will be nominated by the President to serve as
the next Commissioner and Dr. Joshua "Josh" Sharfstein
will serve as the Principal Deputy Commissioner of
the FDA. … The FDA is the premier agency of its kind
in the world, and President Obama wants to revitalize
the agency and empower it to make the best possible
decisions for the American people based on the best
science available. Dr. Hamburg and Dr. Sharfstein will
work hard to support scientific integrity at FDA,
strengthening the ability of the agency's professionals to
do their work on behalf of the American people. They
are the perfect people to translate the President's vision
for the FDA into reality."

We share your vision and we urge that you provide all
necessary support to enable your new leadership to
bring change to FDA without delay as part of your
planned healthcare reform. As stated in a recent NY
Times editorial, you must "send a clear signal to the
bureaucracy that the days of neglect are over. Officials
[must] make clear that the … practice of distorting
science and weakening regulation to favor industry also
is over."

– We completely agree.   FDA must carry out its work

in a transparent manner based on sound science in order to improve the lives of all Americans, reduce health care costs, and expand health care access. Much work remains to be done at FDA and all pending matters need to be addressed. The wrongdoing revealed in the Wall Street Journal involves top FDA officials and requires immediate investigation. Astoundingly, since May 2008, Dr. von Eschenbach, Dr. Torti, Mr. McConagha, and numerous top FDA officials, have been well-aware of other serious wrongdoing, and failed to take any actions, while the physicians and scientists who spoke out and refused to comply have suffered retaliation. The clearance/approval of medical devices that were not made in accordance with the laws, rules and regulations, need to be re-visited.

Furthermore, those FDA employees who have engaged in wrongdoing, who have violated laws, rules, and regulations, who have abused their power and authority, and/or who have engaged in retaliation, should be dealt with swiftly. Immediate and decisive disciplinary action will send a strong message FDA-wide that wrongdoing will no longer be tolerated and those who engage in wrongdoing will be held accountable. Some wrongdoing may be beyond the scope of FDA's jurisdiction and may need referral to the U.S. Attorney General.

All FDA employees who are committed to public integrity, who follow the laws, rules and regulations, who use science to promote public safety and health, and who have the courage and patriotism to speak out , must be protected and must have their professional lives restored. We ask that you accept nothing less.

Sincerely,

(names of scientists signing have been redacted)

This letter is posted on the internet and was pasted into this chapter on judicial and regulatory corruption.

The settlement scam perpetrated upon the Medtronic victims who were fraudulently induced to opt into Medtronic's global settlement fund is detailed in the following relevant pleading:

IN THE UNITED STATES DISTRICT COURT
DISTRICT OF MINNESOTA

IN RE:
Multidistrict Litigation

MEDTRONIC, INC.   No. 08-1905
SPRINT FIDELIS LEADS   (RHK/JSM)
PRODUCTS LIABILITY
LITIGATION

THIS DOCUMENT RELATES TO:
Case No. 10-cv-3373

DONALD K. ALEXANDER,

PLAINTIFF,

VS.

WILLIAM A. HAWKINS, SUSAN ALPERT, KATHLEEN ERICKSON DiGIORNO, STEPHEN N. OESTERLE, M.D., GARY ELLIS, BRIAN RYSDAM, BOONE HOSPITAL CENTER DANIEL ROTHERY, NANCY TUNE, MISSY ARNOLD, AND MEDTRONIC, INC., DEFENDANTS.

PLAINTIFF'S SUGGESTIONS IN RESPONSE TO DEFENDANTS' SUGGESTIONS OPPOSING GRANTING OF PLAINTIFF'S FRCP RULE 60B MOTION

Comes now Plaintiff and submits his suggestions in response to Defendants' suggestions opposing granting of Plaintiff's FRCP Rule 60B motion:

1.   Opposing counsel cleverly substituted as Defendants' Exhibit A the Rule 60B motion Plaintiff filed before Judge Laughrey in Missouri rather than

Plaintiff's Rule 60B motion Plaintiff filed before Judge

Kyle; apparently in an effort to obscure the statement

made by Medtronic's spokesperson, Christopher

Garland, who stated during October 2010 that the

settlement fund amounting to 268 million dollars would

be allocated between approximately 8,100 claimants

who represent virtually all US claims (see The Legal

Reader: Average Medtronic Settlement Is $33,000 --

Squarespace Services services@squarespace.com).

Thus, the 42% increase in the number of settlement fund

participants, the extended delay in fund payout plus the

additional administrative and legal fees charged to said

fund pursuant to an increase of 42% in total claimants

came as a complete surprise to Plaintiff [surprise ---

Rule 60B(1) grounds for relief].

        2.   Defendants' suggestions and supporting

case citations address a FRCP Rule 60B motion

pursuant to a decision on the merits of a case rather than

a voluntary dismissal by Plaintiff in reliance upon a

good faith settlement agreement between Medtronic's

attorneys and Plaintiff's Steering Committee. Opposing

counsel is correct in pointing out that the terms of the

settlement agreement are shrouded in mystery and

timelessness as pertaining to payout allocations by tier

level, timing of payout, and the amount to be held back

for Medicare reimbursement. It is most probable that

not a single Plaintiff imagined the 42% increase in fund

participants, the reduction in the fund from 268 million

to 220 million, and a 40% hold back for insurance

subrogation claims. Such a drastic change without

discussion or agreement with Plaintiffs in the settlement

allocations (as previously described by Medtronic's

spokesperson, Christopher Garland in October 2010,

and which remained unmodified) amounts to massive

deception (bordering on fraud) of Plaintiffs in order to

obtain the dismissal of Plaintiffs' individual suits.

Defendants' suggestions entirely skirt this prima facie

evidence of surprise and deception and ramble on about

the burden of proof to support a FRCP Rule 60B motion

attempting to set aside a ruling on the actual merits of a

case.

3.   Plaintiffs reasonably relied upon the

Plaintiffs' Steering Committee to inform Plaintiffs of

such a drastic change in the number of claimants and the

subsequent reduction in the allocation to each claimant

possible from a fixed fund. The Plaintiffs' Steering

Committee did not disclose the 42% increase in the

number of claimants, the 40% holdback, and the lengthy

delay in payout from the fund until Plaintiffs had

already agreed to dismissal of their cases thus leaving a

FRCP Rule 60B motion as the only route to opting out

of the settlement after the massive reductions in

Plaintiffs allocations were announced.

4.   Defendants' exhibits have zero bearing on

the issues raised in Plaintiff's Rule 60B motion but

cover case background which is not disputed by Plaintiff

thereby serving only to mask suggestions in opposition

to granting of Plaintiff's motion which do not address

the substance of Plaintiff's alleged grounds for relief.

Respectfully submitted,

Donald Alexander
31057 Oak Ridge Drive

Rocky Mount, Missouri 65072
(573) 365-7782   donalexander557@gmail.com

CERTIFICATE OF SERVICE

The undersigned hereby certifies that a true and complete copy of Plaintiff's foregoing RESPONSIVE PLEADING was forwarded on January 18, 2012 by US Mail, first class postage prepaid, to Jonathan H. Garside, Fox Galvin Law Firm L.L.C., One South Memorial Drive, Twelfth Floor, St. Louis, MO 63102; and to Daniel L. Ring, Mayer Brown LLP, 71 South Wacker Drive, Chicago, Illinois 60606

Donald K. Alexander, Plaintiff

The foregoing legal pleadings examples were selected because each pleadings involves Medtronic, Incorporated.

CHAPTER TWO

Bribery, conspiracy, murder and dereliction of duty

The following Civil RICO suit filed against Medtronic details a known portion of the bribery, conspiracy, murder and public fraud committed by Medtronic management pursuant to which numerous senior citizens died and tens of thousands were seriously injured:

IN THE UNITED STATES DISTRICT COURT
WESTERN DISTRICT OF MISSOURI
CENTRAL DIVISION

DONALD K. ALEXANDER,) CASE No. 2:10-4081-cv-c-NKL

PLAINTIFF,   ) Civil RICO

VS.   ) Suit

WILLIAM A. HAWKINS, SUSAN)

ALPERT, KATHLEEN ERICKSON   ) JURY TRIAL

DiGIORNO, STEPHEN N. OESTERLE,) REQUESTED

M.D., GARY ELLIS, MEDTRONIC)

OPERATING ROOM EMPLOYEES,   )

AND MEDTRONIC INCORPORATED,   )

    DEFENDANTS.   )

PLAINTIFF'S AMENDED COMPLAINT AND CIVIL RICO CLAIM PLEADING STATEMENT

PLAINTIFF'S AMENDED CLAIM FOR DAMAGES PURSUANT TO VIOLATIONS OF FEDERAL CIVIL RICO STATUTE; PURSUANT TO FALSE ADVERTISING AND CONSUMER FRAUD; PURSUANT TO EMPLOYER VICARIOUS LIABILITY; AND PURSUANT TO CONSPIRACY AMONG JOINT TORTFEASORS ---- FOR A TOTAL OF FOUR COUNTS IN COMPLAINT

Comes now Plaintiff Donald K. Alexander and in support of the above captioned complaint states to the Court:

1.   This is an action to recover damages inflicted upon Plaintiff by Defendants in violation of Title 18 U.S.C. Section 1962(c) & (d) and pursuant to Section 1964(c) [RICO Statute]; for damages pursuant to false advertising and consumer fraud prohibited under state tort laws; pursuant to criminal conspiracy among members of Medtronic, Incorporated's (hereinafter

"Medtronic") management team; and pursuant to employer vicarious liability.

2.   At all times and dates referred to herein pertaining to the property/financial damages inflicted upon Plaintiff by Defendants, Plaintiff was a Missouri Citizen residing in Morgan County, Missouri at 31057 Oak Ridge Drive, Rocky Mount, Missouri 65072.

3.   During the specific times and dates referred to herein pertaining to the pattern of criminal acts which resulted in said damages inflicted upon Plaintiff pursuant to a criminal conspiracy proscribed by Title 18 U.S.C. Section 1962(c) & (d), Defendants William A. Hawkins, Susan Alpert, Kathleen Erickson DiGiorno, Stephen N. Oesterle, M.D., and Gary Ellis, were employed by Medtronic and functioning in various upper management positions at Medtronic (the RICO enterprise and instrumentality by which the Defendants named in this paragraph inflicted property/financial injuries upon Plaintiff). An employee and/or agent of Medtronic was performing programming and testing

functions in the operating rooms at the hospital where Plaintiff was implanted with a Medtronic cardiac device known to said Medtronic employee and/or agent to be potentially defective, extremely dangerous, and perhaps fatal at the time of Plaintiff's said implanting.

4.   During the specific times and dates referred to herein Defendant Medtronic was routinely doing business in Missouri advertising, marketing, distributing and assisting with implanting of Medtronic implantable cardiac devices. Medtronic's corporate offices were located at 710 Medtronic Parkway, Minneapolis, Minnesota 55432.

JURISDICTION AND VENUE STATEMENT

5.   The Missouri county of Morgan is located within the jurisdiction of the United States District Court for the Western District of Missouri, Central Division. The United States District Courts have original jurisdiction of civil claims brought pursuant to Title 18 U.S.C. 1962. Therefore, jurisdiction and venue are proper in the United States District Court for the Western District of Missouri, Central Division.

6.   A defective and dangerous dual chamber Medtronic pacemaker and defibrillator, known to Medtronic and to Medtronic's employees/agents to be defective, dangerous and perhaps fatal, was sold under false pretenses to Plaintiff by Medtronic on July 6, 2007 and implanted into Plaintiff with the direct assistance of a Medtronic employee/agent.

7. <u>COUNT ONE: PROPERTY & FINANCIAL DAMAGES PURSUANT TO VIOLATION OF TITLE 18 U.S.C. 1962(c), and 1962(d)</u>

The Medtronic cardiac device implanted into Plaintiff as the direct and proximate result of a pattern of intentional criminal acts on the part of members of Medtronic's management team, named as Defendants herein, was a Medtronic dual chamber pacemaker and defibrillator equipped with a Sprint Fidelis lead recalled by Medtronic on October 15, 2007.

8.   During the past ten years, members of Medtronic's management team named as Defendants herein have established multiple bribery schemes,

informant and witness retaliation, wire and mail fraud, financial institution fraud, and murder (by knowingly causing the deaths of numerous individuals implanted with cardiac devices known to said Defendants to be defective thereby demonstrating total disregard for human life), plus various other state and federal crimes including perjury and criminal false advertising as a pattern of criminal acts incorporated into Medtronic's routine method of conducting business. Said pattern of criminal behavior has been repeatedly documented by investigations conducted by law enforcement agencies, court proceedings and public records compiled by the United States Department of Justice; The United States District Courts sitting in Minneapolis, Memphis, and the North District of California; Federal Judge James Rosenbaum; and US Senator Charles Grassley as reported by the Associated Press, the Wall Street Journal, The New York Times and other national and local news media.

9.   Although Medtronic has settled criminal allegations by paying out millions, said pattern of

criminal acts have brought in billions in sales for Medtronic while avoiding billions in defective inventory losses and producing billions in pretax profits. Because said pattern of criminal acts have resulted in multiple deaths while demonstrating total and reckless disregard for human life, several of the Defendants named herein are indictable for 3rd degree murder under Minnesota's, Missouri's, and other states' murder statutes (Missouri Revised Statute 565.020: "A person commits the crime of murder in the second degree if he knowingly causes the death of another person.......;" ---- Minnesota Statute 609.195(a): "Whoever, without intent to effect the death of any person, causes the death of another by perpetrating an act eminently dangerous to others and evincing a depraved mind, without regard for human life, is guilty of murder in the third degree and may be sentenced to imprisonment for not more than 25 years").

10.   Internal Medtronic documents filed pursuant to discovery rules during law suits presided over by the United States District Courts in Tennessee, California,

and Massachusetts, and various state courts reveal the details of the vigorous campaigns that some of the Defendants herein set up to unlawfully influence doctors.   The documents show that Medtronic made bribery payments of at least fifty million dollars to health care providers.   The US Department of Justice reports that Medtronic was flagrantly involved in multiple bribery schemes during 2003 through 2006. On July 19, 2006, the US Department of Justice issued a press release stating that over a period of five years (1998 through 2003) Medtronic paid kickbacks in a number of ways including sham consulting agreements, sham royalty agreements, and lavish trips to desirable locations; and that these patently illegal kickbacks violated the Anti-kickback Statute and the False Claims Act .

     11.   Medtronic conducts business and ships its medical devices including pacemakers and defibrillators throughout the United States and around the world. Medtronic has repeatedly withheld critical defective product information from the public and intentionally

dumped billions of dollars worth of defective inventories into the stream of interstate commerce. In February 2005, Medtronic, after being accused of said dumping, finally notified approximately 87,000 individuals that their Medtronic defibrillator might fail. However, company documents filed in a California Lawsuit for the North District of California, Randall v. Medtronic, case number C-05-3707-JW show that Medtronic management knew about the flaw in the defibrillators and continued to sell the defective implants for two more years. Apparently, the lucrative bribery schemes made health care providers including Boone Hospital Center blind, deaf and dumb.

12.   Public records (FDA MAUDE data base); studies conducted by health care providers (such as Minneapolis Heart Institute); medicals journals (such as Heart Rhythm publications); doctors (such as Dr. Sidney Wolfe and Dr. Robert Hauser); and watchdog organizations (such as Public Citizen) had been warning health care providers for six months prior to July 6,

2007 that the Sprint Fidelis leads were faulty, dangerous, and unnecessarily and repeatedly shocking and injuring heart patients implanted therewith such that numerous patient deaths were plainly foreseeable.

13.   Dr. Robert Hauser at the Minneapolis Heart Institute conducted studies on the Sprint Fidelis leads, and both published his findings in HEART RHYTHM medical journal (in March 2007) and warned Medtronic as well as the FDA (in February 2007) that the leads were fracturing at an unacceptable rate and should be removed from the market. As an integral part of said multiple bribery schemes, Medtronic's management team members named as Defendants herein induced both health care providers and heart patients needing defibrillators (see Medtronic's 100 million dollars mass media campaign directed to potential recipients of implanted defibrillators initiated in January, 2007) to proceed with implanting Medtronic defibrillators which said Defendants absolutely knew were potentially defective, extremely dangerous and foreseeably would certainly cause the premature death

of some of the recipients implanted therewith (at least thirteen such premature deaths have been admitted by Medtronic management and over one hundred have been reported – (see FDA MAUDE data base).

14.   Medtronic was cited by Federal Judge James Rosenbaum for dumping tens of thousands of defibrillators know to Medtronic management to be defective and possibly fatal into the stream of interstate commerce between March 2003 and February 2005. Medtronic had, according to Judge Rosenbaum, withheld critical defective Medtronic product information during 2003 from both FDA and the general public when applying for pre-market approval (intentional perjury) to place a battery known to be defective and perhaps fatal into new cardiac implant models being introduced into the stream of interstate commerce.

15.   Moreover, Medtronic had, according to US Senator Charles Grassley, between January 2007 and October 15, 2007 intentionally dumped defibrillators

known to Medtronic management to be potentially defective and possibly fatal to recipients thereof into the stream of interstate commerce; and Medtronic had, according to Senator Grassley, in January 2007 intentionally engaged in a false and fraudulent advertising campaign promoting these same defibrillators.

16.   The foregoing enumerated criminal acts during the past ten years involved the same victims (individuals needing implanted defibrillators); the same pattern of criminal acts (bribes, kickbacks, retaliation against informants and witnesses, mail and wire fraud pertaining to false FDA reporting and fraudulent claims submitted to Medicare, financial institution fraud pertaining to raiding the public treasury funding false Medicare claims, and knowingly causing multiple deaths). Thus, the predicate criminal acts demonstrate both continuity and interrelationship and most certainly could not have been carried out without a conspiracy to do so between Defendants Hawkins, Alpert, DiGiorno, Oesterle, and Ellis. The ultimate goal of said conspiracy

was to increase Medtronic's market share thereby increasing corporate net profits and increasing the conspiring individuals' bonus opportunities, stock option values, salaries and benefits plus career advancement at the expense of injuring and killing numerous individuals implanted with Medtronic cardiac devices known to the conspirators to be potentially defective, extremely dangerous and fatal to some recipients thereof. Because Medtronic paid out mere millions in cash settlements to the US Department of Justice in lieu of criminal prosecution and to victims of Medtronic's pattern of criminal behavior while raking in billions in profits during the most recent ten years, Medtronic was emboldened to continue said pattern of criminal behavior as its routine method of conducting business; and such a lopsided ratio of cash settlements to profits creates the high probability that Medtronic will resort to the same pattern of criminal behavior in the future.

17.   Defendant William A. Hawkins has served as

Chief Executive Officer of Medtronic and Chairman of the Board since August, 2008. Between May 2004 and August, 2008, Hawkins served as President and Chief Operating Officer of Medtronic. Between January 2002 and May 2004, he served as Senior Vice President and President of Medtronic's Vascular Business. Thus, common sense dictates that the above described pattern of criminal acts and supporting conspiracy involving other members of Medtronic's management team (named as Defendants herein) could not possibly have been carried out without Defendant Hawkins' knowledge and approval.

18. Defendant Susan Alpert served as Vice President of Regulatory Affairs and Compliance of Medtronic from July 2003 until her recent promotion to Senior Vice President and Chief Regulatory Officer overseeing all Medtronic global regulatory efforts. Defendant Kathleen Erickson DiGiorno accepted an upper management position with Medtronic in 1998 and currently serves, since 2006, as Vice President, Chief Ethics and Compliance Officer reporting to Defendant

Hawkins. Prior to 2006, one of her primary responsibilities involved investigation into potential anti-kickback and Medicare fraud issues. Defendants Alpert and DiGiorno knowingly and intentionally acted in furtherance of said criminal conspiracy by continuously ignoring the pattern of criminal acts involving bribery, kickbacks and dumping of cardiac implants known to be defective, extremely dangerous and perhaps fatal into the stream of interstate commerce.

19. Defendant Steven N. Oesterle, M.D. has served as Medtronic's Senior Vice President for Medicine and Technology since 2002 providing executive leadership for scientific research, formation of technological strategies and developing relationships with the world's medical communities. As detailed above, the relationships developed with the medical communities by Defendant Oesterle included kickbacks and other bribes.

20. Defendant Gary Ellis has served as Medtronic's Senior Vice President and Chief Financial

Officer since May 1, 2005. Between 1989 and 2005 he served as Assistant Corporate Controller and other roles in corporate finance. Therefore, it is certain that Defendant Ellis knew of and was involved in the payout of more than fifty million dollars in illegal bribes and kickbacks.

21.   Plaintiff,   having   been   knowingly, intentionally, willfully, wantonly and recklessly, with total disregard for Plaintiff's very life, exposed to and implanted with a defibrillator known to said conspirators to be potentially defective and perhaps fatal, has suffered actual monetary damages in the bare minimum amount of $72,000.00 (purchase of defective defibrillator and related implantation services billed to Plaintiff) plus substantial non-economic damages which are not being claimed under this COUNT ONE. Plaintiff's said financial damages to his property (money) are the direct and proximate result of the flagrant violations of Title 18 U.S.C. Section 1962(c) and 1962(d) on the part of said conspirators as set forth above. But for the pattern of criminal acts on the part of

said conspirators, Plaintiff would not have purchased and subsequently been implanted with said Medtronic defibrillator and thus would not have suffered the above described property/financial damages.

22.   Subpoenaed documents and public records from the US Department of Justice; the federal courts; from investigating authorities; from the FDA; from Medtronic's internal records; from Senator Grassley's office; plus numerous depositions to be procured by Plaintiff of individuals having specific first hand knowledge of the foregoing facts and circumstances will prove by the preponderance of such admissible evidence that the Defendants named herein have repeatedly violated 18 U.S.C. Section 1962(c) and (d) and have inflicted property/financial damages upon Plaintiff and thousands of other individuals in the same victim category as Plaintiff --- individuals in need of implanted defibrillators.

23.   The faulty Sprint Fidelis lead which carries between 700 and 1,000 volts directly to Plaintiff's heart

is screwed to Plaintiff's cardiac tissue. The faulty lead cannot be removed without risk of sudden cardiac death and is partially blocking the electrical lead access to Plaintiff's heart such that another lead alongside the faulty Sprint Fidelis lead would compound the blockage problem. In addition, Plaintiff's risk of death in connection with said defective implant has more than quadrupled because the Sprint Fidelis lead fracture rate is increasing with time since implanting. Medtronic, under intense pressure from the medical community and the FDA, finally recalled Plaintiff's Medtronic implant by serial number on October 15, 2007.

24. According to medical journals and independent studies by watchdog organizations as reported by the New York Times and the Wall Street Journal, currently one in ten individuals implanted with the faulty Medtronic Sprint Fidelis leads will suffer inappropriate multiple shocks stopping their hearts and/or causing cardiac injuries which can be fatal; and, worse yet, the Sprint Fidelis fracture rate is expected to accelerate to an astounding thirty percent of such leads

implanted. Consequently, Plaintiff and thousands of other individuals implanted with said leads are living in constant fear and anxiety due to the Medtronic time bomb screwed to their hearts.

WHEREFORE, Plaintiff respectfully prays this Honorable Court to enter judgment against Defendants Hawkins, Alpert, DiGiorno, Oesterle, and Ellis jointly and severally; and for an award of treble damages (3 x $72,000.00 = $216,000.00) plus costs of suit, and reasonable attorneys' fees as authorized by Title 18 U.S.C. Section 1964(c); and for such additional and further relief as the Court deems just and proper.

25. COUNT TWO: CRIMINAL CONSPIRACY IN VIOLATION OF TITLE 18 U.S.C. 1962(d):

Plaintiff hereby incorporates the foregoing paragraphs (1) through (24) as if fully set forth in this COUNT TWO. As detailed in Count One, Defendants knew or had reason to know that Medtronic defibrillators equipped with Sprint Fidelis leads were potentially defective, extremely dangerous and fatal to some of the recipients thereof; and that Medtronic management had adopted bribery, perjury, false advertising, fraud upon the FDA, and withholding of critical defective product information from the FDA and potential recipients of defibrillator implants. By acquiescing in said pattern of criminal behavior, each member of Medtronic's management team named as Defendants herein acted in furtherance of the criminal conspiracy being perpetrated by Medtronic's executive level management to intentionally dump into the stream of interstate commerce defective defibrillator inventory known to be defective, dangerous and perhaps fatal to individuals implanted therewith.

26.   With respect to this COUNT TWO, medical facilities and physicians are the "association-in-fact RICO enterprise" through which Medtronic management carried out the schemes to sell to persons suffering from serious heart arrhythmias potentially defective, extremely dangerous and sometimes fatal defibrillators. Therefore, for the purpose of this COUNT

TWO, the aforementioned "association-in-fact" encompassing physicians and health care facilities is the RICO enterprise such that Medtronic can be named as a Defendant. Medtronic's liability in this COUNT TWO flows from vicarious liability for the acts of its employees acting in furtherance of said conspiracy through which Plaintiff suffered actual and compensatory damages.

27. But for the tortious acts carried out against Plaintiff by Defendants as described in this COUNT TWO in furtherance of said conspiracy described in the foregoing paragraphs, Plaintiff would not have suffered actual and compensatory damages including emergency and intensive care medical treatment pursuant to repetitive inappropriate shocking episodes, increased risk of death, blockage of arterial access to Plaintiff's heart, depression, anxiety, mental terror, sleeplessness, and restriction of physical activities.

WHEREFORE, Plaintiff respectfully prays this

Honorable Court to enter judgment under COUNT TWO against Defendants jointly and severally, and for an award of actual financial damages in an amount to be determined by the trier-of-facts, and for an award of compensatory damages in an amount to be determined by the trier-of-facts. In addition, because said damages were inflicted upon Plaintiff intentionally, willfully, wantonly, and with total disregard for Plaintiff's life, Plaintiff further prays this Honorable Court for an award of punitive damages in proportion to Defendants' wealth and in sufficient amount to dissuade others similarly situated from like conduct.

28.   COUNT THREE: VICARIOUS LIABILITY ON THE PART OF MEDTRONIC, INC. FOR THE TORTIOUS ACTS AGAINST PLAINTIFF CARRIED OUT BY ITS EMPLOYEE/AGENT ASSISTING WITH PLAINTIFF'S IMPLANTATION WITH A DEFECTIVE, DANGEROUS AND PERHAPS FATAL DEFIBRILLATOR

Plaintiff hereby incorporates the foregoing paragraphs (1) through (27) as if fully set forth in this COUNT THREE. A Medtronic employee/agent was present in Plaintiff's hospital operating room when Plaintiff was implanted with said defective, dangerous and perhaps fatal Medtronic defibrillator. Said employee/agent programmed and helped test fire Plaintiff's Medtronic pacemaker/defibrillator implanted into Plaintiff's chest and wired to Plaintiff's heart with a Sprint Fidelis lead screwed to Plaintiff's cardiac tissue.

29.   Because said Medtronic employee/agent routinely programs and test fires implanted Medtronic defibrillators; and because said employee/agent routinely interrogates defective Medtronic defibrillators equipped with the deadly Sprint Fidelis leads; and because said employee/agent reprograms Medtronic defibrillators equipped with Sprint Fidelis leads; said employee/agent was intimately familiar with the full range of quality problems surrounding said deadly leads. Consequently, said employee/agent knew or certainly had reason to know that said leads were fracturing at an unacceptable rate; that the fracture rate was increasing geometrically with the passing of time since being

implanted; that removal of said leads carried a high risk of sudden cardiac death; that hundreds of people implanted with said deadly leads had been injured and/or suffered repetitive inappropriate shocking episodes; that said deadly leads had already killed several individuals; and that Medtronic, Inc. through its employees and agents had been withholding critical safety information from the FDA and the general public, it is absolutely certain that said employee/agent knew that Plaintiff's cardiac health as well as Plaintiff's very life was being put in jeopardy by implantation of said Medtronic defibrillator equipped with said Sprint Fidelis lead.

30.   But for said tortious acts carried out against Plaintiff by said Medtronic employee/agent, Plaintiff would not have suffered the actual and compensatory damages described by Plaintiff in the foregoing paragraphs.

31.   It is black letter law that a corporation has vicarious liability for the tortious acts committed by its employees and agents while carrying out the routine

business of the corporation. Therefore, liability attaches to Medtronic, Inc. for the tortious acts committed against Plaintiff by said employee/agent assisting with Plaintiff's implantation of said Medtronic defibrillator equipped with a Sprint Fidelis lead.

WHEREFORE, Plaintiff respectfully prays this Honorable Court to enter judgment under this COUNT THREE against Defendant Medtronic, and for an award of actual financial damages as set forth in the foregoing paragraphs in an amount to be determined by the trier-of-facts. In addition, Plaintiff prays this Honorable Court for an award of compensatory damages for personal injuries described in the foregoing paragraphs in an amount to be determined by the trier-of-facts. Because the damages described in this COUNT THREE were inflicted upon Plaintiff intentionally, willfully, wantonly, and with total disregard for Plaintiff's life, and with Medtronic's foreknowledge, Plaintiff prays this Honorable Court for an award of punitive damages in proportion to

Medtronic's'   wealth and in sufficient amount to dissuade others similarly situated from like conduct; and for such additional relief as this Honorable Court deems just and proper.

32. <u>COUNT FOUR: INTENTIONAL FALSE ADVERTISING AND CONSUMER FRAUD</u>

Plaintiff hereby incorporates the foregoing paragraphs (1) through (31) as if fully set forth in this COUNT FOUR. Concerning the pattern of criminal acts on the part of Medtronic management employees, including false advertising and consumer fraud, Senator Charles Grassley from Iowa wrote to Defendant Hawkins:

"As a senior member of the United States Senate..........I have a special responsibility to protect the health of Medicare and Medicaid beneficiaries and safeguard taxpayer dollars authorized by Congress for these programs.........In carrying out this duty, I have been investigating various aspects of the medical

industry, including the substantial financial ties between the device industry and practicing physicians. I have also been examining the safety and cost of devices that are sold to the American public. As the largest medical device company in the United States, the practices of Medtronic, Inc. (Medtronic) have a profound impact on healthcare. Recently, several articles in the New York Times reported that Medtronic warned doctors to stop using a potentially faulty lead attached to your heart defibrillators. This defect has caused malfunctions in hundreds of patients and may have contributed to five deaths. What I find troubling is that Medtronic took months to stop the sales of the faulty lead even though the problem has been reported in a peer review journal months prior. This study found over 500 complaints of adverse events with this particular lead that were reported in the FDA's MAUDE data between September 2004 and January 2007. Certainly this data was also available to executives at Medtronic. However, Medtronic took no apparent action to inform doctors *and patients of the potential risks. Meanwhile, it was reported by the Chicago Tribune that Medtronic launched a $100 million marketing campaign in January to advertise its heart defibrillators, some of which used the faulty leads."*

33.   In this October 16, 2007 letter directed to William A. Hawkins, CEO, Medtronic, Inc., Senator Grassley accused Medtronic management of withholding from the medical community and general public critical safety information adverse to Medtronic while directing a massive advertising campaign aimed directly at potential recipients of cardiac implants to persuade such potential recipients to be implanted with Medtronic defibrillators which Medtronic absolutely knew were potentially defective and extremely dangerous and could result in the untimely death of the individuals implanted with said defibrillators. Under state laws such false advertising is felonious.

34.   The one hundred million dollars mass media advertising campaign launched by Medtronic management in January 2007 dubbed "What's Inside"

included a commercial in which a soft voice promises viewers and listeners that inside the Medtronic defibrillators they'll find "10,000 more kisses" and saying "it will always be there for you close to your heart with power to restart it in case of sudden cardiac arrest."

35. Federal Judge James M. Rosenbaum on November 28, 2006 issued a formal opinion in which he stated:

"Sometime in early 2003, during routine laboratory testing, Medtronic discovered a defect in the CHI 4420L battery which caused it to discharge prematurely. Medtronic's engineers continued to test the CHI4420L between February and September of 2003....... Medtronic did not notify the FDA or the medical community of this discovery, even though it had identified, and known for six months, a defect which could cause its defibrillators to lose their electrical charge in days instead of years.........Medtronic began to redesign its CHI 4420L battery to address the defect in

the spring of 2003.......While this redesign was under way, Medtronic sought and obtained approval for three additional device models -- the Maximo DR and VR ICDs and Insync II Protect -- each containing the CHI 4420L battery. Each device's PMA Supplement application failed to advise the FDA of the CHI 4420's documented shorting problem, or that this anomaly could lead to premature depletion. Thus, these new devices received FDA approval, and went into production and distribution with a battery Medtronic knew could short and discharge prematurely ....Sometime between February and April, 2004, Medtronic began to receive field reports of premature battery depletion.........By December, 2004, more than one year and nine months after its own discovery of the problem, Medtronic received nine field returns of devices with premature battery depletion. Even with this field report in hand, it was not until February, 2005 --two full years after its own discovery of the battery discharge anomaly ---that Medtronic first warned the public of the defective battery."

36.   Withholding   critical   product   safety information from the public and fraudulent advertising is "business as usual" for Medtronic, Inc.   Judge Rosenbaum's   opinion   documents   that   Medtronic continued to manufacture and sell cardiac devices to be implanted in heart patients which Medtronic knew for two full years contained defective batteries that could deplete in a matter of days and result in the death of the recipients when the implanted device failed to deliver the life saving shock to correct fatal heart fibrillation. It is not known how many people Medtronic sent to their deaths (due to incomplete field reporting and intentional concealment) with Medtronic implants which Medtronic knew were potentially defective, extremely dangerous and   perhaps   fatal;   and   Medtronic   continues   to intentionally conceal   this adverse information from both the FDA and the general public by false reporting on the number of deaths and serious injuries caused by its   defective   Sprint   Fidelis   defibrillator   leads   and

defective CHI 4420L defibrillator batteries. Medtronic simply does not know the number of deaths and serious injuries caused by said pattern of criminal behavior because: bribed physicians are not likely to report patient deaths as being due to defective Medtronic defibrillators; funeral homes and morticians are not qualified to detect or analyze defective cardiac implants; many heart patients who die pursuant to heart fibrillation will be assumed dead in spite of their defibrillator's proper functioning because only the individual who died would know whether the defibrillator failed; in the absence of autopsy by a qualified expert in cardiac implants, the individual killed by a defective Medtronic defibrillator would be quietly laid to rest; and Medtronic has admitted to investigative reporters that Medtronic does not bother to track such deaths but rather relies upon adverse field reports which encompass an unknown fraction of those killed by defective Medtronic defibrillators. Medtronic has admitted to at least thirteen deaths due to said faulty Medtronic defibrillators. The actual number will most likely run into the hundreds.

37. Since 2005, partial and incomplete reporting (subject to intentional concealment on the part of Medtronic) indicates that over twenty thousand recipients of Medtronic defibrillators containing defective CHI 4420L batteries or Sprint Fidelis leads have undergone replacement surgery; over thirty-five hundred patients have been injured and/or repeatedly shocked and their hearts repeatedly stopped; and more than a hundred have reportedly died thus far (according to non-Medtronic sources). The injury and death rate is expected to skyrocket as the Sprint Fidelis fracture rate increases with time. Some cardiac implant analysts predict a fracture rate of roughly thirty percent during the fourth year following implantation. Medtronic, Inc. has finally notified over eighty-seven thousand recipients of Medtronic defibrillator implants that their defibrillators may malfunction and cause injury or death.

38. Plaintiff not being knowledgeable

concerning cardiac implants reasonably relied on Medtronic's advertising of the quality, safety and reliability of its defibrillators to Plaintiff's detriment. Plaintiff's actual and compensatory damages as described herein and future related medical expenses plus Plaintiff's escalating risk of death are the direct and proximate result of said false advertising and consumer fraud on the part of Medtronic, Inc. acting through its management team. But for said false advertising and consumer fraud on the part of Medtronic, Plaintiff would never have consented to be implanted with a Medtronic pacemaker defibrillator known to Medtronic management to be potentially defective, extremely dangerous and possibly fatal, nor would Plaintiff have such a time bomb wired to his heart causing Plaintiff continuous anxiety, depression, sleeplessness, mental trauma and periodic mental terror.

THEREFORE, in view of the allegations stated herein and in attached RICO Pleading Statement, and all of the documented facts supporting said allegations,

Plaintiff prays this Honorable Court for judgment against Defendant Medtronic, Inc. and for an award of actual damages in an amount to be determined by the trier-of-facts; and for an award of compensatory damages as deemed appropriate by the trier-of-facts and this Honorable Court to compensate Plaintiff for pain and suffering; for anxiety and depression; for sleeplessness; for periodic mental terror; for increased risk of death; for partial blockage of normal access to Plaintiff's heart for a pacemaker or defibrillator; and for future medical expenses in connection with the defective Medtronic defibrillator lead screwed to Plaintiff's heart.

In addition, because said criminal false advertising and consumer fraud on the part of Medtronic management as described herein was knowing, intentional, reckless, wanton, and with total disregard for Plaintiff's life, Plaintiff further prays this Honorable Court for an award of punitive damages in proportion to Defendant Medtronic, Inc.'s wealth and in sufficient amount to dissuade others similarly situated from like conduct; and for such other and further relief as the Court deems just and proper.

PLAINTIFF'S RICO CLAIM PLEADING STATEMENT

Comes now Plaintiff and files Plaintiff's RICO Claim Pleading Statement and by reference thereto incorporates said statement into Plaintiff's Amended Complaint in the above captioned cause of action. Said pleading statement addresses specifics of factual allegations to be heard and decided by a jury as set forth in Plaintiff's Amended Complaint and includes federal case citations specifying a well pled Civil RICO complaint.

In order for a Civil RICO claim to get past summary judgment motions and before a jury, case law dictates that:

*   The criminal behavior complained of must impact interstate commerce in some demonstrable manner.

*   Defendants must have within the most recent ten years violated at least two of the felonies enumerated in the Civil RICO statute.

*   A pattern of criminal behavior must be evident that results in financial damages to the plaintiff and to others similarly situated.

*   There must be a reasonable possibility that the pattern of criminal behavior might be repeated in the future.

*   The criminal behavior must have inflicted financial damages on more than one individual who represent a "class of intended victims."

*   There must be continuity and interrelation between the criminal acts complained of and the financial damages claimed.

*   There must be a RICO enterprise such as an identifiable business entity and/or an "Association in Fact" (loosely knit group of individuals or organizations through which the pattern of criminal behavior has been carried out).

*   Defendants need not be convicted of the complained of criminal   behavior but only be indictable under state law for predicate crimes for which the

penalty is at least one year imprisonment, or for predicate criminal acts enumerated in the Federal RICO Statute.

The Civil RICO statute of limitations is four years.

The Civil RICO Statute is a perfect fit for Medtronic, Inc. because:

Medtronic's cardiac implants and spinal fusion kits are marketed in every state and 126 foreign countries and enter the stream of interstate commerce directly from the manufacturing site.

Medtronic's management team has engaged in a pattern of criminal behavior during the most recent ten years and such criminal acts have injured the same class of victims (people being medically treated with Medtronic medical devices along with Medicare false claims which raid the public treasury). Such individuals have suffered significant and measurable financial damages.

There is very obvious continuity and interrelationship between the pattern of criminal behavior and the financial damages claimed.

Medtronic, by its own actions, has demonstrated repeatedly that the complained of criminal behavior might be repeated in the future.

The victims (same class of victims) number over 75,000.

Medtronic, Inc. could legally serve as the RICO enterprise; or the doctors and hospitals which cooperated with Medtronic's various bribery schemes and Medicare fraud would certainly qualify as "an Association in Fact" thereby constituting the RICO enterprise through which Medtronic carried out the alleged pattern of criminal behavior such that Medtronic could be named as a Defendant and incur liability.

Medtronic's senior management team is definitely indictable for bribery, mail and wire fraud, financial institution fraud, retaliation against informants, whistleblowers and witnesses, and murder (the enumerated felonies committed by Medtronic management described with specificity herein).

During the most recent ten years, Medtronic has repeatedly engaged in criminal activities; and has been cited by a federal judge and a US senator for knowingly dumping billions of dollars worth of defective cardiac implants into the stream of interstate commerce.

Numerous individuals have died as the direct result of this intentional dumping of defective implants into the stream of interstate commerce with certain foreknowledge on the part of Medtronic management that the defective implants would kill some patients implanted therewith. Such intentional dumping demonstrates depraved minds and reckless disregard for human life which constitutes murder in the second or third degree punishable by twenty to twenty-five years imprisonment in some states (see Amended Complaint, pg. 6, par. 9).

The evidence necessary to get the Civil RICO claim to the jury already exists and is well documented by law enforcement agencies, the federal courts and Senator Charles Grassley; and said documentation is available either as public records or in a form subject to subpoena.

Title 18 U.S.C. Section 1962 refers to defendants as "persons," and only those defendants who are named as persons under section 1962 can be held liable for violations of Civil RICO. A defendant "person" can be an individual or corporation - it makes no difference so long as the defendant person engaged in a pattern of criminal activity. Parties often confuse the defendant "person" with the RICO enterprise and equate the RICO enterprise with a criminal enterprise. Many times, the RICO enterprise is an enterprise that perpetrates crime (e.g., a Mafia family), but many other times the RICO enterprise may be the victim of the criminal activity or a passive instrument of the defendants' criminal acts. *See National Organization for Women v. Scheidler*, 510 U.S. 249, 259 n.5 (1994), *Reves v. Ernst & Young*, 507 U.S. 170, 184 (1993) ("[a]n enterprise . . . might be 'operated' or 'managed' by others 'associated with' the enterprise who exert control over it as, for example, by bribery").

Thus, an "association in fact" can be the RICO enterprise even though it is a totally innocent victim. Naming an entity as simply a RICO enterprise does not impose any liability on that entity. *United States v. Philip Morris USA, Inc.*, 566 F.3d 1095 (D.C. Cir. 2009). Banks, law firms, insurance companies, and advertising agencies that unknowingly facilitate a defendant's criminal activities are often named as the Rico enterprise or part of the enterprise through which the defendant conducted his pattern of racketeering.

Simply stated, to establish a Civil Rico claim under 1962(c), the Plaintiff must prove that a defendant person was employed by or associated with an enterprise that engaged in or affected interstate commerce and that the defendant person operated or managed the enterprise through a pattern of racketeering activity, and that the Plaintiff was injured in Plaintiff's business or property by reason of the pattern of racketeering activity. The RICO enterprise may be an illegal entity such as a Mafia family or a legal entity such as a corporation; or a loose-knit group of people or

legal entities referred to under the Civil RICO statute as
an "association-in-fact enterprise" such as physicians
and hospitals through which a defendant person carried
out a pattern of criminal activity affecting interstate
commerce. *United States v. Turkette, 452 U.S. 576, 580-
81; 18 U.S.C. Section 1961(4).* The majority of 1962(c)
violations are carried out through an "association-in-fact
enterprise" when a major corporation is involved.
*Phillip Morris USA, Inc. 566 F.3(d) at 1111; Boyle v.
United States, 129 S.Ct. 2237 (2009).* Consequently, in
Plaintiff's foregoing Amended Complaint, Medtronic,
Inc. is the RICO enterprise in Counts One and Two;
conspiring physicians and hospitals are the RICO
enterprise in Counts Three and Four; and mass media
outlets are the RICO enterprise in Count Five.   Under
the *Boyle decision the* US Supreme Court defines an
"association-in-fact RICO enterprise" as having three
essential characteristics when engaging in a pattern of
criminal behavior --- purpose, relationship or association
between members, and sufficient longevity. These three

essential characteristics are obvious in the association-
in-fact relationship between Medtronic and health care
providers. Medtronic, Inc., a legal "person," can
logically carry out a pattern of criminal behavior
through physicians and hospitals which are separate and
distinct from Medtronic such that Medtronic can be
named as a Defendant when carrying out its criminal
activities through physicians and hospitals; or through
mass media outlets. *Living Designs, Inc. v. E.I. Dupont
De Nemours and Co., 431 F.3(d)353, 362 (9th Cir.
2005); River City Markets, Inc. v. Fleming Foods West,
Inc., 960 F.2(d) 1458, 1461 (9th Cir. 1992).* The Section
1962(c) requirement that the defendant person "conduct
or participate, directly or indirectly, in the conduct of
such enterprises affairs," was clarified in *Reeves v. Ernst
& Young, 507 U.S. 170, 183 (1993)* by a holding that
such conducting or participating is not limited to upper
management and is a question of fact for the jury to
decide.

    In *H.J. Inc. v. Northwestern Bell, 492 U.S. 229
(1989)* the US Supreme Court ruled that the factors of

relatedness and continuity combine to produce a pattern
of racketeering. Medtronic demonstrated this pattern by
the relatedness and continuity involving bribing
physicians and hospitals making possible the wire and
mail fraud connected with fraudulent Medicare claims
involving unnecessary hospital admissions and
knowingly dumping defective defibrillators into the
stream of interstate commerce resulting in the deaths of
numerous persons in order to perpetrate fraud upon a
financial institution by raiding the public treasury
funding Medicare and retaliating against informants,
whistle-blowers and witnesses who tried to expose the
racketeering activity. Medtronic defrauded Medicare by
knowingly billing Medicare for cardiac implants known
to Medtronic to be defective, dangerous and perhaps
fatal, and by conspiring with physicians and hospitals to
intentionally overcharge Medicare for spinal treatments
by keeping patients in the hospital for an outpatient
procedure.

Medtronic concealed its pattern of criminal

behavior by outright perjury and withholding defective product information from FDA and the general public and by spending a hundred million in false advertising promoting the reliability and safety of the defective cardiac implants being dumped into the stream of interstate commerce. Medtronic's unbelievable success in bribing health care providers combined with dumping defecting inventories and ripping off Medicare to raid the public treasury while foreseeing the deaths of numerous persons implanted with defective defibrillators (murder) and reaping billions in profits after paying cash settlements to victims and government agencies emboldened Medtronic to keep dumping defective defibrillators into the stream of interstate commerce whereby Plaintiff was financially injured on July 6, 2007 (money charged for defective defibrillator and related medical services).

Continuity (the possibility that the criminal behavior pattern may be repeated in the future) is demonstrated by the circumstance surrounding the past criminal activities, and/or a series of related predicate criminal acts committed over an extended period of time (generally defined by the courts as two years or more). *Spool v. World Child Intern Adoption Agency, 520 F.3(d) 178, 184 (2nd Cir. 2008).* In addition, penalties imposed weighed against profits realized may result in the future repetition of the past criminal behavior pattern. Medtronic's pattern of criminal behavior spanned ten years and resulted in billions of profit dollars in exchange for a few hundred million in penalties and law suit settlements.

Regardless of whether a Civil RICO claim is based on federal or state criminal statutes or a combination thereof, it is not required that a conviction be obtained in connection with the alleged criminal activity. It is entirely sufficient to maintain the Civil RICO action if the criminal activity is indictable. *S.P.R.L. v. Imrex, Co., 473 U.S. 479, 493 (1985).* As detailed above and at page (6), par. (9) of Plaintiff's Amended Complaint, Medtronic's management team members named as Defendants are indictable for all of the predicate criminal acts alleged including murder.

Medtronic's pattern of criminal behavior over the most recent ten years has been flagrant and arrogant and has been challenged by law enforcement agencies, members of the US Congress, physicians not tainted by Medtronic bribes, whistleblower law suits, medical journals, watchdog organizations, class action law suits, and investigative reporters. Both national and local news media have covered the investigation of and reporting of allegations of crimes committed by Medtronic's management team and the internet is brimming with similar public information.

Medtronic's management team members have thus far escaped criminal prosecution by Medtronic paying out a few hundred million dollars in fines and settlement of victims' law suits while at the same time Medtronic has reaped several billion dollars in pretax profits directly attributable to Medtronic's said pattern of criminal behavior. Based on FDA oversight and FDA pre-market approval of Medtronic's defective defibrillators, the federal courts have protected

Medtronic by ruling that federal law administered through the FDA and other regulatory agencies preempts state law tort actions founded upon product liability theories of recovery thereby barring the courts to thousands of individuals injured by Medtronic's defective medical devices and survivors of those killed by Medtronic. Thus, at the present time, civil suits based upon criminal behavior provide the only legal theory of recovery for Medtronic's victims.

The names of other individuals in the same victim class as Plaintiff number into the tens of thousands and thus are too numerous to list in this statement. However, such names are readily available in the list of plaintiffs contained in law suits involving Medtronic's defective defibrillator batteries and defective defibrillator leads presided over by Judge James Rosenbaum and Judge Richard Kyle in the US District Court for the District of Minnesota.

FDA and other regulatory federal agencies are vulnerable to huge bribes and have been charged with massive corruption as well as negligence and dereliction of regulatory duties. In August 2009, numerous internet news media websites reported that Dr. Daniel Schultz resigned from his post as the head of the FDA's medical devices division pursuant to charges by nine FDA scientists who wrote letters to President Obama wherein the scientists alleged there was "systematic corruption and wrongdoing that permeates all levels of FDA," including within the medical device approval process, which put the safety of Americans at risk. The scientists claim they were pressured to approve certain devices and the careers of those who refused to do so were threatened. In one egregious example, the scientists claimed that Dr. Schultz approved a Regan Biologics knee repair device in 2008 despite the scientists' repeated rejections of the device because it posed "an increased risk" in comparison to similar devices. The Government Accountability Office in January 2009 criticized the FDA, saying the agency had not been inspecting the production of medical devices as regularly as it was required to do. High risk devices, such as pacemakers and defibrillators were supposed to be inspected every two years but the agency had been inspecting such high risk devices only every six years. Medtronic's deadly Sprint Fidelis defibrillator leads were never tested other than bench trials and were not subjected to any scrutiny by the FDA even after hundreds of heart patients had been seriously injured. Such official negligence, indifference, sloppiness and dereliction of regulatory duties (probably pursuant to rampant bribery) no doubt emboldened Medtronic to adopt a pattern of criminal behavior as detailed herein as its normal course of conducting business.

Medtronic, of course, denies any instance of criminal activity and gives the general public false and intentionally misleading facts and figures which amount to smoke and mirrors to convince past and future victims that black is white, up is down, and evil is good; but the true facts paint a far difference scenario. Even now, prior to Plaintiff's discovery and subpoenaed documents, there exists a preponderance of evidence in

secure and public records to indict Medtronic
management for the predicate criminal activity detailed
herein; and there is certainly sufficient justification for
the defendants named in the foregoing Amended
Complaint to answer to a civil jury. Plaintiff's
complaint is not founded upon product liability issues
but rather upon a pattern of criminal behavior proscribed
within *18 U.S.C. Sections 1961 through 1964.*

On July 18, 2006, the *US Department of Justice*
issued a press release reporting that Medtronic had
agreed to pay forty million dollars to settle allegations
that Medtronic paid illegal kickbacks to physicians to
induce them to use and endorse Medtronic's spinal
products medical devices and that the illegal kickbacks
involved sham consulting agreements, sham royalty
agreements, and lavish trips to desirable locations.
Internal Medtronic documents filed in connection with
whistleblower law suits confirm that Medtronic paid out
over fifty million dollars in bribes to illegally influence
physicians and other health care providers to use and
recommend Medtronic's medical devices. *Poteet v.*

Medtronic, 03-2979, 07-5262, US District Court,

Western District of Tennessee, Poteet v. Lawrence G.

Lenke, MD, 07-10237, US District Court, District of

Massachusetts, Poteet, 552 F.3(d) at 508. See also 31

U.S.C. Section 3730(e)(4).

According to wrongful termination allegations by
former Medtronic employees, Medtronic has practiced
retaliation against informants and witnesses.   *A*
ruling handed down by the US Sixth Circuit in No. 07-
5262, United States and Poteet v. Medtronic included
this dictum: "On October 5, 2001, Scott Wiese
("Wiese"), a former Regional Sales Manager for
Medtronic's MSD Division, filed a wrongful termination
suit against Medtronic, MSD, and others in superior
court in Los Angeles, California. Wiese alleged that he
had been fired because he had refused to comply with
his supervisors' directives to pay illegal kickbacks and
bribes to MSD's physician customers in exchange for
their business. To support this claim, his complaint
described in detail MSD's alleged practice of providing

doctors with extravagant travel arrangements, sham

consulting agreements, and company-sponsored "Think

Tanks" to ensure their continued use of MSD products.

On September 11, 2002, John Doe ("Doe"),[2] a former

MSD attorney, filed a qui tam action under the FCA

against Medtronic, MSD, and ten named physicians in

the United States District Court for the Western District

of Tennessee.   The complaint alleged that MSD had

used improper sales and marketing tactics to induce the

defendant physicians to use MSD products in violation

of the FCA and the federal Anti-Kickback statute, 42

U.S.C. § 1320a-7b(b).[3] In particular, Doe claimed that

MSD had provided the physicians with numerous

kickbacks -- free marketing services, sham consulting,

research, and royalty agreements, lavish all-expense-

paid trips to vacation resorts, and limousine service to

adult entertainment clubs-in exchange for the

physicians' continued use of MSD products and their

promoting of MSD products among their fellow doctors.

According to Doe, "[t]hese improper inducements

inherently taint[ed] the claims for payment submitted by

providers for MSD products and [thereby] cause[ed]
the submission of false claims for payment in violation
of the [FCA]." J.A. at 396.   In addition to the damages
and civil penalties provided by the FCA, Doe also
sought relief under state and federal law for Doe's
allegedly retaliatory discharge from MSD."

In the wrongful termination suit filed by former
Medtronic Attorney Ami P. Kelly, in the US District
Court in Memphis, the suit alleged that Medtronic
routinely entertained physicians with visits to a popular
strip club and the services of prostitutes.

The most egregious of the criminal acts engaged
in by Medtronic during the most recent ten years were
bribery, perjury, criminal false advertising via telephone,
mail and mass media outlets, plundering of Medicare
and the public treasury, and murder in connection with
foreseeable multiple deaths triggered by defective
cardiac implants which Medtronic management
absolutely knew were defective, extremely dangerous
and fatal to a predictable percentage of recipients

implanted therewith.

Federal Judge James Rosenbaum accused Medtronic of perjury before the FDA and knowingly dumping defective defibrillators into the stream of interstate commerce for approximately two years (2003-2005). It is unknown how many people died from fatal heart fibrillation when their defibrillator failed to function due to a defective Medtronic battery but Medtronic admits that over nineteen thousand individuals underwent replacement surgeries for which Medicare paid the overwhelming majority of the cost in addition to paying for the defective defibrillators; and over eighty thousand individuals are still at risk of sudden cardiac death due to the defective batteries according to Medtronic's in-house estimate. Thus, Medtronic's fraudulent dumping of said defibrillators into an unsuspecting national market cost Medicare and the public treasury funding Medicare hundreds of millions of dollars thus far.

U.S. Senator Charles Grassley accused Medtronic of criminal false advertising via telephone, mail and mass media while at the same time intentionally dumping defibrillators known to Medtronic to be defective into interstate commerce for six months during 2007. More than a hundred people were reportedly killed by the defective defibrillators (25 have now been admitted by the FDA and Medtronic) and thousands have been injured. Here again, Medicare and the public treasury were raided by Medtronic. The truly devastating effect of Medtronic's Sprint Fidelis lead fraud is yet to be consummated. According to independent sources and studies conducted by doctors at the University of Rochester, the Minneapolis Heart Institute, the Mayo Clinic, Heart Rhythm Medical Journal, and the University of Ottawa Heart Institute, the Medtronic Sprint Fidelis defibrillator leads fracture rate now exceeds twenty percent for implant recipients under fifty years of age, more than twelve percent for older patients, and is expected to reach an astounding average of thirty percent for all age groups during the fourth year following implantation. The death toll will be staggering and the cost to Medicare and the public treasury will be devastating.

Respectfully submitted,

Donald K. Alexander, Plaintiff

Donald Alexander
31057 Oak Ridge Drive
Rocky Mount, Missouri 65072
(573) 557-2114   donalexander557@gmail.com

As patently demonstrated in the foregoing Civil RICO suit and pleading statement, federal regulatory and law enforcement authorities have gobbled up more than 100 million dollars doled out by Medtronic to bribe the US Department of Justice to back off from low key investigations into Medtronic's pattern of criminal behavior.

Considering the felonious nature of Medtronic's documented pattern of criminal behavior, why has the FBI not bothered to pursue indictments against Medtronic's management team for such flagrant criminal behavior affecting interstate commerce? It is most obvious that when a major corporation is throwing around hundreds of millions in bribes and hush payments, law and order doesn't count for much. Why has the news media not been raising the issue of dereliction of duties on the part of federal law enforcement authorities? Why has there been no formal investigation by a Congressional Committee? What's going on here, folks? These crimes were not committed under the cover of darkness or in obscure back rooms but rather before the eyes of the FBI, US Department of Justice, the FDA, the US Attorney General, State Attorney Generals, US Senators, Federal Judges and both local and national news media.

Apparently, it is politically permissible to murder senior citizens indiscriminately when the hands that serve the public are full of Medtronic's cash.

CHAPTER THREE

Federal preemption of state laws when medical
devices manufacturers are sued for damages
inflicted by defective products

In the opinion handed down by Judge Richard
Kyle in which he absolved Medtronic, Incorporated
from any and all liability for intentionally killing
numerous senior citizens and injuring tens of thousands
of other seniors, Judge Kyle basically rewrote the
United States Supreme Court decision rendered in
Riegel v. Medtronic. There exists probable cause that in
exchange for his judicial brilliance Judge Kyle was
handsomely enriched by Medtronic.   What is this
probable cause?

First, Judge Kyle, contrary to the cherished
premise that federal judges shun even the appearance of
a conflict of interest, refused to recuse himself from

presiding over the "Medtronic Sprint Fidelis Products Liability Litigation involving over 10,000 individual suits consolidated for discovery and pretrial motions in the US District Court for the District of Minnesota. The potential liability facing Medtronic was astronomical. Judge Kyle desperately clung to the multi-district litigation (MDL) thereby remaining in a position to order the dismissal of all the product liability cases for which Medtronic was on the hook. Why?? The Plaintiffs' lawyers filed a motion for recusal. Alexander filed a motion for recusal. Judge Kyle dismissed the motions and saw no conflict of interest connected with his son working for a law firm and holding stock in the firm which was heavily involved with Medtronic's legal affairs. Now, isn't that interesting?

Second, Judge Kyle denied motions to remand to the court where originally filed a Civil RICO suit against Medtronic over which Judge Kyle had zero subject matter jurisdiction. Why?? Is he a legal moron? Probably not. Then why?? Could it have been a massive increase in his personal wealth?

Third, Judge Kyle set an entirely new precedent in American jurisprudence by granting total immunity against state law torts filed against Medtronic by the survivors of the folks murdered by Medtronic and the tens of thousands seriously injured by Medtronic's criminal behavior. Judge Kyle opined that only the FDA has proper authority to oversee Medtronic's corporate wrongdoing regardless of how many people Medtronic kills and injures. And, of course, this was during the very same time window that nine FDA scientists were complaining to President Obama by personal letter that the FDA was totally corrupt and unable to protect the health and safety of the American people with respect to medical device manufacturers. Moreover, during the same time window, Medtronic was being investigated for Medicare fraud and mass bribery of health care providers.

Why would Judge Kyle during the above described time window be so adamant about throwing a complete blanket of federal preemption around

Medtronic?? Perhaps, Judge Kyle's flash of judicial enlightenment was unearthed by the Riegel v. Medtronic US Supreme Court decision. The actual text of the Riegel decision appears below:

128 S.Ct. 999 (2008)

Donna S. RIEGEL, individually and as administrator of the Estate of Charles R. Riegel, Petitioner,

v.

MEDTRONIC, INC.

No. 06-179.

Supreme Court of United States.

Argued December 4, 2007.

Decided February 20, 2008.

1002*1002 Allison M. Zieve, Washington, DC, for petitioner.

Theodore B. Olson, Washington, D.C., for respondent.

Edwin S. Kneedler, Washington, DC, for the United States as amicus curiae, by special leave of the Court, supporting the respondent.

Wayne P. Smith, Schenectady, NY, Allison M. Zieve, Counsel of Record, Brian Wolfman, Scott L. Nelson, Public Citizen Litigation Group, Washington, DC, for Petitioner.

Kenneth S. Geller, David M. Gossett, Andrew E. Tauber, Mayer Brown LLP, Washington, D.C., Theodore B. Olson, Counsel of Record, Matthew D. Mcgill, Amir C. Tayrani, Dace A. Caldwell, Gibson, Dunn & Crutcher LLP, Washington, D.C., for Respondent.

Justice SCALIA delivered the opinion of the Court.

We consider whether the pre-emption clause enacted in the Medical Device Amendments of 1976, 21 U.S.C. § 360k, bars common-law claims challenging the safety and effectiveness of a medical device given premarket approval by the Food and Drug Administration (FDA).

The Federal Food, Drug, and Cosmetic Act (FDCA), 52 Stat. 1040, as amended, 21 U.S.C. § 301 *et seq.,* has long required FDA approval for the introduction of new drugs into the market. Until the statutory enactment at issue here, however, the introduction of new medical devices was left largely for the States to supervise as they saw fit. See *Medtronic, Inc. v. Lohr,* 518 1003*1003 U.S. 470, 475-476, 116 S.Ct. 2240, 135 L.Ed.2d 700 (1996).

The regulatory landscape changed in the 1960's and 1970's, as complex devices proliferated and some failed. Most notably, the Dalkon Shield intrauterine device, introduced in 1970, was linked to serious infections and several deaths, not to mention a large number of pregnancies. Thousands of tort claims followed. R. Bacigal, The Limits of Litigation: The Dalkon Shield Controversy 3 (1990). In the view of many, the Dalkon Shield failure and its aftermath demonstrated the inability of the common-law tort system to manage the risks associated with dangerous devices. See, *e.g.,* S. Foote, Managing the Medical Arms Race 151-152 (1992). Several States adopted regulatory measures, including California, which in 1970 enacted a law requiring premarket approval of medical devices. 1970 Cal. Stats. ch. 1573, §§ 26670-26693; see also Leflar & Adler, The Preemption Pentad: Federal Preemption of Products Liability Claims After Medtronic, 64 Tenn. L.Rev. 691, 703, n. 66 (1997) (identifying 13 state statutes governing medical devices as of 1976).

Congress stepped in with passage of the Medical Device Amendments of 1976(MDA), 21 U.S.C. § 360c *et seq.,* [11]which swept back some state obligations and imposed a regime of detailed federal oversight. The MDA includes an express pre-emption provision that states:

"Except as provided in subsection (b) of this section, no State or political subdivision of a State may establish or continue in effect with respect to a device intended for human use any requirement—"(2) which relates to the safety or effectiveness of the device or to any other matter included in a requirement applicable to the device under this chapter." § 360k(a).

The exception contained in subsection (b) permits the FDA to exempt some state and local requirements from peemption.

The new regulatory regime established various levels of oversight for medical devices, depending on the risks they present. Class I, which includes such devices as elastic bandages and examination gloves, is subject to the lowest level of oversight: "general controls," such as labeling requirements. § 360c(a)(1)(A); FDA, Device Advice: Device Classes, http://www.fda. gov/cdrh/devadvice/3132.html (all Internet materials as visited Feb. 14, 2008, and available in Clerk of Court's case file). Class II, which includes such devices as powered wheelchairs and surgical drapes,*ibid.*, is subject in addition to "special controls" such as performance standards and postmarket surveillance measures, § 360c(a)(1)(B).

The devices receiving the most federal oversight are those in Class III, which include replacement heart valves, implanted cerebella stimulators, and pacemaker pulse generators, FDA, Device Advice: Device Classes, *supra.* In general, a device is assigned to Class III if it cannot be established that a less stringent classification would provide reasonable assurance of safety and effectiveness, and the device is "purported or represented to be for a use in supporting or sustaining human life or for a use which is of substantial importance in preventing impairment of human health," or "presents a potential unreasonable risk of illness or injury." § 360c(a)(1)(C)(ii).

1004*1004 Although the MDA established a rigorous regime of premarket approval for new Class III devices, it grandfathered many that were already on the market. Devices sold before the MDA's effective date may remain on the market until the FDA promulgates, after notice and comment, a regulation requiring premarket approval. §§ 360c(f)(1), 360e(b)(1). A related provision seeks to limit the competitive advantage grandfathered devices receive. A new device need not undergo premarket approval if the FDA finds it is "substantially equivalent" to another device exempt from premarket

approval. § 360c(f)(1)(A). The agency's review of
devices for substantial equivalence is known as the §
510(k) process, named after the section of the MDA
describing the review. Most new Class III devices enter
the market through § 510(k). In 2005, for example, the
FDA authorized the marketing of 3,148 devices under §
510(k) and granted premarket approval to just 32
devices. P. Hutt, R. Merrill, & L. Grossman, Food and
Drug Law 992 (3d ed.2007).

Premarket approval is a "rigorous" process. _Lohr_ 518
U.S., at 477, 116 S.Ct. 2240. A manufacturer must
submit what is typically a multivolume application.
FDA, Device Advice—Premarket Approval (PMA) 18,
http://www.fda.gov/cdrh/ devadvice/pma/printer.html. It
includes, among other things, full reports of all studies
and investigations of the device's safety and
effectiveness that have been published or should
reasonably be known to the applicant; a "full statement"
of the device's "components, ingredients, and properties
and of the principle or principles of operation"; "a full

description of the methods used in, and the facilities and controls used for, the manufacture, processing, and, when relevant, packing and installation of, such device"; samples or device components required by the FDA; and a specimen of the proposed labeling. § 360e(c)(1). Before deciding whether to approve the application, the agency may refer it to a panel of outside experts, 21 CFR § 814.44(a) (2007), and may request additional data from the manufacturer, § 360e(c)(1)(G).

The FDA spends an average of 1,200 hours reviewing each application, , _and *Lohr, supra,* at 477 grants premarket approval only if it finds there is a "reasonable assurance" of the device's "safety and effectiveness," § 360e(d). The agency must "weig[h] any probable benefit to health from the use of the device against any probable risk of injury or illness from such use." § 360c(a)(2)(C). It may thus approve devices that present great risks if they nonetheless offer great benefits in light of available alternatives. It approved, for example, under its Humanitarian Device Exemption procedures, a ventricular assist device for children with failing hearts, even though the survival rate of children using the device was less than 50 percent. FDA, Center for Devices and Radiological Health, Summary of Safety and Probable Benefit 20 (2004), online at http://www.fda.gov/cdrh/pdf3/H 030003b.pdf.

The premarket approval process includes review of the device's proposed labeling. The FDA evaluates safety and effectiveness under the conditions of use set forth on the label, § 360c(a)(2)(B), and must determine that the proposed labeling is neither false nor misleading, § 360e(d)(1)(A).

After completing its review, the FDA may grant or deny premarket approval. § 360e(d). It may also condition approval on adherence to performance standards, 21 CFR § 861.1(b)(3), restrictions upon sale or distribution, or compliance with other requirements, § 814.82. The agency is also 1005*1005 free to impose device-specific restrictions by regulation. § 360j(e)(1).

If the FDA is unable to approve a new device in its proposed form, it may send an "approvable letter" indicating that the device could be approved if the applicant submitted specified information or agreed to certain conditions or restrictions. 21 CFR § 814.44(e). Alternatively, the agency may send a "not approvable" letter, listing the grounds that justify denial and, where practical, measures that the applicant could undertake to make the device approvable. § 814.44(f).

Once a device has received premarket approval, the MDA forbids the manufacturer to make, without FDA permission, changes in design specifications, manufacturing processes, labeling, or any other attribute, that would affect safety or effectiveness. § 360e(d)(6)(A)(i). If the applicant wishes to make such a change, it must submit, and the FDA must approve, an application for supplemental premarket approval, to be evaluated under largely the same criteria as an initial application. § 360e(d)(6); 21 CFR § 814.39(c).

After premarket approval, the devices are subject to reporting requirements. § 360i. These include the obligation to inform the FDA of new clinical investigations or scientific studies concerning the device which the applicant knows of or reasonably should know of, 21 CFR § 814.84(b)(2), and to report incidents in which the device may have caused or contributed to death or serious injury, or malfunctioned in a manner that would likely cause or contribute to death or serious injury if it recurred, § 803.50(a). The FDA has the power to withdraw premarket approval based on newly reported data or existing information and must withdraw approval if it determines that a device is unsafe or ineffective under the conditions in its labeling. § 360e(e)(1); see also § 360h(e) (recall authority).

Except as otherwise indicated, the facts set forth in this section appear in the opinion of the Court of Appeals. The device at issue is an Evergreen Balloon Catheter marketed by defendant-respondent Medtronic, Inc. It is a Class III device that received premarket approval from the FDA in 1994; changes to its label received supplemental approvals in 1995 and 1996.

Charles Riegel underwent coronary angioplasty in 1996, shortly after suffering a myocardial infarction. App. to Pet. for Cert. 56a. His right coronary artery was diffusely diseased and heavily calcified. Riegel's doctor inserted the Evergreen Balloon Catheter into his patient's coronary artery in an attempt to dilate the artery, although the device's labeling stated that use was contraindicated for patients with diffuse or calcified stenoses. The label also warned that the catheter should not be inflated beyond its rated burst pressure of eight atmospheres. Riegel's doctor inflated the catheter five times, to a pressure of 10 atmospheres; on its fifth inflation, the catheter ruptured. Complaint 3. Riegel developed a heart block, was placed on life support, and underwent emergency coronary bypass surgery.

Riegel and his wife Donna brought this lawsuit in April 1999, in the United States District Court for the Northern District of New York. Their complaint alleged that Medtronic's catheter was designed, labeled, and

manufactured in a manner that violated New York

common law, and that these defects caused Riegel to

suffer severe and permanent injuries. The complaint

raised a number of common-law claims. The District

Court held that the 1006*1006 MDA pre-empted

Riegel's claims of strict liability; breach of implied

warranty; and negligence in the design, testing,

inspection, distribution, labeling, marketing, and sale of

the catheter. App. to Pet. for Cert. 68a; Complaint 3-4. It

also held that the MDA pre-empted a negligent

manufacturing claim insofar as it was not premised on

the theory that Medtronic violated federal law. App. to

Pet. for Cert. 71a. Finally, the court concluded that the

MDA preempted Donna Riegel's claim for loss of

consortium to the extent it was derivative of the pre-

empted claims. *Id.,* at 68a; see also *id.,* at 75a.[2]

The United States Court of Appeals for the Second

Circuit affirmed these dismissals. 451 F.3d 104 (2006).

The court concluded that Medtronic was "clearly subject

to the federal, device-specific requirement of adhering to the standards contained in its individual, federally approved" premarket approval application. *Id.,* at 118. The Riegels' claims were pre-empted because they "would, if successful, impose state requirements that differed from, or added to" the device-specific federal requirements. *Id.,* at 121. We granted certiorari.[3] 551 U.S. ___, 127 S.Ct. 3000, 168 L.Ed.2d 725 (2007).

Since the MDA expressly pre-empts only state requirements "different from, or in addition to, any requirement applicable ... to the device" under federal law, § 360k(a)(1), we must determine whether the Federal Government has established requirements applicable to Medtronic's catheter. If so, we must then determine whether the Riegels' common-law claims are based upon New York requirements with respect to the device that are "different from, or in addition to" the federal ones, and that relate to safety and effectiveness. § 360k(a).

We turn to the first question. In *Lohr,* a majority of this Court interpreted the MDA's pre-emption provision in a manner "substantially informed" by the FDA regulation set forth at 21 CFR § 808.1(d). 518 U.S., at 495, 116 S.Ct. 2240; see also *id.,* at 500-501,116 S.Ct. 2240. That regulation says that state requirements are pre-empted "only when the Food and Drug Administration has established specific counterpart regulations or there are other specific requirements applicable to a particular device...." 21 CFR § 808.1(d). Informed by the regulation, we concluded that federal manufacturing and labeling requirements applicable across the board to almost all medical devices did not pre-empt the common-law claims of negligence and strict liability at issue in *Lohr.* The federal requirements, we said, were not requirements specific to the device in question— they reflected "entirely generic concerns about device regulation generally." 518 U.S., at 501, 116 S.Ct. 2240. While we disclaimed a conclusion that general federal requirements could never pre-empt, or general state duties never be pre-empted, 1007*1007 we held that no pre-emption occurred in the case at hand based on a careful comparison between the state and federal duties at issue.*Id.,* at 500-501, <u>116 S.Ct. 2240</u>.

Even though substantial-equivalence review under § 510(k) is device specific *Lohr* also rejected the manufacturer's contention that § 510(k) approval imposed device-specific "requirements." We regarded the fact that products entering the market through § 510(k) may be marketed only so long as they remain substantial equivalents of the relevant pre-1976 devices as a qualification for an exemption rather than a requirement. *Id.,* at 493-494, <u>116 S.Ct. 2240</u>; see also *id.,* at 513, <u>116 S.Ct. 2240</u> (O'Connor, J., concurring in part and dissenting in part).

Premarket approval, in contrast, imposes "requirements" under the MDA as we interpreted it in *Lohr.* Unlike general labeling duties, premarket approval is specific to individual devices. And it is in no sense an exemption from federal safety review—it *is* federal safety review.

Thus, the attributes that *Lohr* found lacking in § 510(k)
review are present here. While § 510(k) is "'focused on
equivalence, not safety,'" *id.,* at 493,<u>116 S.Ct. 2240</u>
(opinion of the Court), premarket approval is focused on
safety, not equivalence. While devices that enter the
market through § 510(k) have "never been formally
reviewed under the MDA for safety or efficacy," *ibid.,*
the FDA may grant premarket approval only after it
determines that a device offers a reasonable assurance of
safety and effectiveness, § 360e(d). And while the FDA
does not "'require'" that a device allowed to enter the
market as a substantial equivalent "take any particular
form for any particular reason," *ibid.,* at 493, <u>116 S.Ct.
2240,</u> the FDA requires a device that has received
premarket approval to be made with almost no
deviations from the specifications in its approval
application, for the reason that the FDA has determined
that the approved form provides a reasonable assurance
of safety and effectiveness.

We turn, then, to the second question: whether the Riegels' common-law claims rely upon "any requirement" of New York law applicable to the catheter that is "different from, or in addition to" federal requirements and that "relates to the safety or effectiveness of the device or to any other matter included in a requirement applicable to the device." § 360k(a). Safety and effectiveness are the very subjects of the Riegels' common-law claims, so the critical issue is whether New York's tort duties constitute "requirements" under the MDA.

In *Lohr,* five Justices concluded that common-law causes of action for negligence and strict liability do impose "requirement[s]" and would be pre-empted by federal requirements specific to a medical device. See 518 U.S., at 512, 116 S.Ct. 2240 (opinion of O'Connor, J., joined by Rehnquist, C. J., and SCALIA and THOMAS, JJ.);*id.,* at 503-505, 116 S.Ct. 2240 (opinion of BREYER, J.). We adhere to that view. In interpreting two other statutes we have likewise held that a provision pre-empting state "requirements" pre-empted common-law duties. *Bates v. Dow Agrosciences LLC*, 544 U.S. 431, 125 S.Ct. 1788, 161 L.Ed.2d 687 (2005) found common-law actions to be pre-empted by a provision of the Federal Insecticide, Fungicide, and Rodenticide Act that said certain States "`shall not impose or continue in effect *any requirements* for labeling or packaging in addition to or different from those required under 1008*1008 this subchapter.'" *id.,* at 443, 125 S.Ct. 1788 (discussing 7 U.S.C. § 136v(b); emphasis added). *Cipollone v. Liggett Group, Inc.*, 505 U.S. 504, 112 S.Ct. 2608, 120 L.Ed.2d 407 (1992), held common-law actions pre-empted by a provision of the Public Health Cigarette Smoking Act of 1969, 15 U.S.C. § 1334(b), which said that "[n]o requirement or prohibition based on smoking and health shall be imposed under State law with respect to the advertising or promotion of any cigarettes" whose packages were labeled in accordance with federal law. See 505 U.S., at 523, 112 S.Ct. 2608 (plurality opinion); *id.,* at 548-549, 112 S.Ct. 2608

(SCALIA, J., concurring in judgment in part and dissenting in part).

Congress is entitled to know what meaning this Court will assign to terms regularly used in its enactments. Absent other indication, reference to a State's "requirements" includes its common-law duties. As the plurality opinion said in *Cipollone,* common-law liability is "premised on the existence of a legal duty," and a tort judgment therefore establishes that the defendant has violated a state-law obligation. *Id.,* at 522, 112 S.Ct. 2608. And while the common-law remedy is limited to damages, a liability award "`can be, indeed is designed to be, a potent method of governing conduct and controlling policy.'" *Id.,* at 521, 112 S.Ct. 2608.

In the present case, there is nothing to contradict this normal meaning. To the contrary, in the context of this legislation excluding common-law duties from the scope of pre-emption would make little sense. State tort law that requires a manufacturer's catheters to be safer, but hence less effective, than the model the FDA has approved disrupts the federal scheme no less than state regulatory law to the same effect. Indeed, one would think that tort law, applied by juries under a negligence or strict-liability standard, is less deserving of preservation. A state statute, or a regulation adopted by a state agency, could at least be expected to apply cost-benefit analysis similar to that applied by the experts at the FDA: How many more lives will be saved by a device which, along with its greater effectiveness, brings a greater risk of harm? A jury, on the other hand, sees only the cost of a more dangerous design, and is not concerned with its benefits; the patients who reaped those benefits are not represented in court. As Justice BREYER explained in *Lohr,* it is implausible that the MDA was meant to "grant greater power (to set state standards `different from, or in addition to' federal standards) to a single state jury than to state officials acting through state administrative or legislative lawmaking processes." 518 U.S., at 504, 116 S.Ct. 2240. That perverse distinction is not required or even suggested by the broad language Congress chose in the MDA,[4] and we will not turn somersaults to create it.

The dissent would narrow the pre-emptive scope of the term "requirement" on 1009*1009 the grounds that it is "difficult to believe that Congress would, without comment, remove all means of judicial recourse" for consumers injured by FDA-approved devices. *Post,* at 1015 (opinion of GINSBURG, J.) (internal quotation marks omitted). But, as we have explained, this is exactly what a pre-emption clause for medical devices does by its terms. The operation of a law enacted by Congress need not be seconded by a committee report on pain of judicial nullification. See, *e.g., Connecticut Nat. Bank v. Germain, 503 U.S. 249, 253-254, 112 S.Ct. 1146, 117 L.Ed.2d 391 (1992)*. It is not our job to speculate upon congressional motives. If we were to do so, however, the only indication available— the text of the statute—suggests that the solicitude for those injured by FDA-approved devices, which the dissent finds controlling, was overcome in Congress's estimation by solicitude for those who would suffer without new medical devices if juries were allowed to apply the tort law of 50 States to all innovations.[5]

In the case before us, the FDA has supported the position taken by our opinion with regard to the meaning of the statute. We have found it unnecessary to rely upon that agency view because we think the statute itself speaks clearly to the point at issue. If, however, we had found the statute ambiguous and had accorded the agency's current position deference, the dissent is correct, see *post,* at 1016, n. 8, that—inasmuch as mere *Skidmore* deference would seemingly be at issue—the degree of deference might be reduced by the fact that the agency's earlier position was different. See *Skidmore v. Swift & Co.,* 323 U.S. 134, 65 S.Ct. 161, 89 L.Ed. 124 (1944); *United States v. Mead Corp.,* 533 U.S. 218, 121 S.Ct. 2164, 150 L.Ed.2d 292 (2001); *Good Samaritan Hospital v. Shalala,* 508 U.S. 402, 417, 113 S.Ct. 2151, 124 L.Ed.2d 368 (1993). But of course the agency's earlier position (which the dissent describes at some

length, *post,* at 1015-1016, and finds preferable) is even
more compromised, indeed deprived of all claim to
deference, by the fact that it is no longer the agency's
position.

The dissent also describes at great length the experience
under the FDCA with respect to drugs and food and
color additives. *Post,* at 1016-1018. Two points render
the conclusion the dissent seeks to draw from that
experience—that the pre-emption clause permits tort
suits— unreliable. (1) It has not been established (as the
dissent assumes) that no tort lawsuits are pre-empted by
drug or additive approval under the FDCA. (2) If, as the
dissent believes, the pre-emption clause permits tort
lawsuits for medical devices just as they are (by
hypothesis) permitted for drugs and additives; and if, as
the dissent believes, Congress wanted the two regimes
to be alike; Congress could have applied the pre-
emption clause to the entire FDCA. It did not do so, but
instead wrote a pre-emption clause that applies only to
medical devices.

The Riegels contend that the duties underlying negligence, strict-liability, and implied-warranty claims are not pre-empted even if they impose "'requirements,'" because general common-law duties are not requirements maintained "'with respect to devices.'" Brief for Petitioner 34-36. Again, a majority of this Court suggested otherwise in *Lohr* See 518 U.S., at 504-505, 116 S.Ct. 2240 (opinion of BREYER, J.); *id.,* at 514, 116 S.Ct. 2240 (opinion of 1010*1010 O'Connor, J., joined by Rehnquist, C. J., and SCALIA and THOMAS, JJ.).[6] And with good reason. The language of the statute does not bear the Riegels' reading. The MDA provides that no State "may establish or continue in effect *with respect to a device ... any requirement*" relating to safety or effectiveness that is different from, or in addition to, federal requirements. § 360k(a) (emphasis added). The Riegels' suit depends upon New York's "continu[ing] in effect" general tort duties "with respect to" Medtronic's catheter. Nothing in the statutory text suggests that the pre-empted state requirement must apply *only* to the relevant device, or only to medical devices and not to all products and all actions in general.

The Riegels' argument to the contrary rests on the text of an FDA regulation which states that the MDA's preemption clause does not extend to certain duties, including "[s]tate or local requirements of general applicability where the purpose of the requirement relates either to other products in addition to devices (e.g., requirements such as general electrical codes, and the Uniform Commercial Code (warranty of fitness)), or to unfair trade practices in which the requirements are not limited to devices." 21 CFR § 808.1(d)(1). Even assuming that this regulation could play a role in defining the MDA's pre-emptive scope, it does not provide unambiguous support for the Riegels' position. The agency's reading of its own rule is entitled to substantial deference, see *Auer v. Robbins*, 519 U.S. 452, 461, 117 S.Ct. 905, 137 L.Ed.2d 79 (1997), and the FDA's view put forward in this case is that the regulation does not refer to general tort duties of care, such as those underlying the claims in this case that a device was designed, labeled, or manufactured in an unsafe or ineffective manner. Brief for United States as *Amicus Curiae* 27-28. That is so, according to the FDA, because the regulation excludes from pre-emption requirements that relate only incidentally to medical devices, but not other requirements. General tort duties of care, unlike fire codes or restrictions on trade practices, "directly regulate" the device itself, including its design. *Id.,* at 28. We find the agency's explanation less than compelling, since the same could be said of general requirements imposed by electrical codes, the Uniform Commercial Code, or unfair-trade-practice law, which the regulation specifically excludes from pre-emption.

Other portions of 21 CFR § 808.1, however, support the agency's view that § 808.1(d)(1) has no application to this case (though still failing to explain why electrical codes, the Uniform Commercial Code or unfair-trade-practice requirements are different). Section 808.1(b) states that the MDA sets forth a "general rule" pre-empting state duties "having the force and effect of law (whether established by statute, ordinance, regulation, *or court decision*)....." (Emphasis added.) This sentence is far more comprehensible under the FDA's view that § 808.1(d)(1) has no application here than under the Riegels' view. We are aware of no duties established by court decision other than common-law duties, and we are aware of no common-law duties that relate solely to medical devices.

1011*1011 The Riegels' reading is also in tension with the regulation's statement that adulteration and misbranding claims are pre-empted when they "ha[ve] the effect of establishing a substantive requirement for a specific device, e.g., a specific labeling requirement" that is "different from, or in addition to" a federal requirement. § 808.1(d)(6)(ii). Surely this means that the MDA would pre-empt a jury determination that the FDA-approved labeling for a pacemaker violated a state common-law requirement for additional warnings. The Riegels' reading of § 808.1(d)(1), however, would allow a claim for tortious mislabeling to escape pre-emption so long as such a claim could also be brought against objects other than medical devices.

All in all, we think that § 808.1(d)(1) can add nothing to our analysis but confusion. Neither accepting nor rejecting the proposition that this regulation can properly be consulted to determine the statute's meaning; and neither accepting nor rejecting the FDA's distinction between general requirements that directly regulate and those that regulate only incidentally; the regulation fails to alter our interpretation of the text insofar as the outcome of this case is concerned.

State requirements are pre-empted under the MDA only to the extent that they are "different from, or in addition to" the requirements imposed by federal law. § 360k(a)(1). Thus, § 360k does not prevent a State from providing a damages remedy for claims premised on a violation of FDA regulations; the state duties in such a case "parallel," rather than add to, federal requirements. *Lohr*, 518 U.S., at 495, 116 S.Ct. 2240; see also *id.*, at

513, 116 S.Ct. 2240 (O'Connor, J., concurring in part and dissenting in part). The District Court in this case recognized that parallel claims would not be preempted, see App. to Pet. for Cert. 70a-71a, but it interpreted the claims here to assert that Medtronic's device violated state tort law notwithstanding compliance with the relevant federal requirements, see *id.,* at 68a. Although the Riegels now argue that their lawsuit raises parallel claims, they made no such contention in their briefs before the Second Circuit, nor did they raise this argument in their petition for certiorari. We decline to address that argument in the first instance here.

* * *

For the foregoing reasons, the judgment of the Court of Appeals is

Affirmed.

After wading through all the legal jargon and pure judicial bafflegab, what the law passed by Congress actually states is this:

"Except as provided in subsection (b) of this section, no State or political subdivision of a State may establish or continue in effect with respect to a device intended for human use any requirement— **which is different from, or in addition to, any requirement applicable under this chapter to the device, and "(2) which relates to the safety or effectiveness of the device or to any other matter included in a requirement applicable to the device under this chapter." § 360k(a).**

Simply stated in non-legal language, what Congress said is that state law cannot impose upon any medical device manufacturer any law or regulation that is contrary to the manufacturing, packaging, and labeling requirements established by FDA pre-market approval for the medical device in question. If the state law or regulation underlying the civil suit is the same as or simply parallel to the pre-market approval specifications imposed by the FDA there is no federal preemption because there is nothing to preempt.

Judge Kyle in his puzzling zeal to protect Medtronic from any and all suits against Medtronic founded upon a state law or regulation, regardless of whether or not such state law or regulation differed from FDA pre-market specifications, basically eliminated all product liability suits against a manufacturer of medical devices. Why?? It is not good law. Neither is it even sensible. The FDA cannot protect the American public health or safety. However they can be easily bribed. That is what the letter to Obama from nine FDA scientists was all about. How big was Judge Kyle's bribe?? The way Medtronic tosses around bribe cash, Kyle may have been enriched by several million dollars. Would Judge Kyle actually take such a bribe? The strange way he buried Alexander's Civil RICO suit against Medtronic under stalled and totally unrelated product liability litigation certainly points in that direction.

Judge Nanette Laughrey, who has demonstrated her propensity for shucking her oath to report professional misconduct on the part of other Missouri Bar members when a seat on the federal bench is up for grabs, sent Alexander's Civil RICO case filed in her court to Judge Kyle. The US Judicial Panel on Multi-district Litigation overruled Alexander's timely filed objections to such transfer to accommodate Judges Laughrey and Kyle in total contradiction to statutory, case and procedural law. Why?? These federal judges are not stupid, just dishonorable. But, alas that is how the legal fraternity totally controls our legal system for the benefit of politically connected lawyers and judges who want to advance their legal careers by appointment to a higher court with the aid and financial assistance of their favorite politically connected law firms.

Such vested interests and lack of integrity are hard to cope with if one has a weak stomach and vomits easily. Nevertheless, that is the legal system we are currently stuck with. The challenge becomes how to cope with such transparent corruption. That is what the two remaining chapters will address.

CHAPTER FOUR

What citizens need to know in order to act as their own attorney and where to find the required information

This book was not written to provide information to criminal defendants. However, one piece of advice is easy to state: Do not expect any justice if you are hauled into court represented only by an appointed attorney or tax supported public defender.

Civil suits will generally involve personal injuries (tort law), contract law, property law, landlord/tenant law, probate law, civil rights, tax law, bankruptcy law, small claims court, and family law. There are other categories of civil law but the vast majority of civil cases will involve the law categories listed above.

Other than small claims court, jurisdiction and venue where the civil claim must be filed will depend upon what category of law is involved. Municipal courts are slightly more complex courts than small claims court. In small claims court, jurisdiction is based upon a claim in the $5,000 or less dollar range. Venue in small claims court is where claims must be filed based upon where the plaintiff(s) and defendant(s) reside.

Municipal courts are city or town courts which handle mainly traffic cases and other misdemeanors like shoplifting, peace disturbance, etc. In municipal courts the defendants usually represent themselves and the municipal judge will control the entire court proceeding. There may or may not be a local prosecutor depending upon the size of the city or town. Municipal courts are basically criminal courts where the defendants are all charged with some misdemeanor violation and the penalty is usually a graduated fine schedule. If jail time is a possibility, the case is usually tried in the associate circuit court where a jury trial can be conducted.

Small claims court operate much like a municipal court where the plaintiff (person filing the claim) and the defendant (person opposing the claim) represent themselves before a judge who questions both plaintiff and defendant and examines any evidence submitted by the opposing parties; then rules on the claim (a "Judge Judy" type court hearing).

Large and populous cities will have a small claims court, a municipal court, an associate circuit court and a circuit court. Family court, probate court and juvenile court will usually be special courtrooms within the associate circuit court or the circuit court. Federal tax courts, bankruptcy courts, and US District courts are part of the federal court system. Federal courts are located within federal judicial districts and are generally located within large urban areas.

There are multiple federal courts in most states. Missouri, for example, has six federal district courts and two federal bankruptcy courts. Jurisdiction is based upon subject matter before the court; and venue is based on where the parties reside or where the events occurred which gave rise to the complaint filed. Jurisdiction is thus determined by subject matter whereas venue is determined by the residence of the parties before the court or where the complained of acts actually occurred. For example: an automobile accident occurring in Morgan County, Missouri involving residents of Morgan County would be heard and decided in the Morgan County Circuit Court located in Versailles, Missouri (the "county seat" for Morgan County). The Morgan County Circuit Court would have both jurisdiction and venue.

A breach of contract case involving a contract signed in Columbia, Missouri and later breached in Eldon, Missouri could be heard and decided in either the Circuit Court for Boone County located in Columbia, Missouri; or in the Circuit Court for the county where Eldon, Missouri is situated. Eldon, Missouri is located in Miller County, Missouri. The county seat for Miller County is located in Tuscumbia, Missouri. If the defendant (the person charged with the breach of contract) lives in Cole County, Missouri and the plaintiff (the individual suing for breach of contract) lives in Camden County, Missouri, the case could also be filed, heard and decided in the Circuit Court for Cole County, Missouri (the county where the defendant may be found). If the defendant does not object, the case could also be filed, heard and decided in the Circuit Court for Camden County, the county where the plaintiff resides. Thus, the plaintiff (the person filing the suit) can choose to file in Boone County Circuit Court, or the Miller County Circuit Court, or the Cole County Circuit Court. And, if the defendant does not object, the plaintiff could also file suit in Camden County.

Any Missouri county circuit court has subject matter jurisdiction over a breach of contract between two different Missouri Citizens. The circuit courts in Boone County, Miller County and Cole County would also be proper venue for the breach of contract suit. Venue would be proper in Camden County only with the defendant's acquiescence.

So, why is the issue of venue important? Perhaps for several reasons that mirror the ease with which our legal system can be manipulated. For example: the judge most likely to be assigned the case in Boone County is overly sympathetic to small businesses. The judge most likely to be assigned the case in Miller County in a rabid liberal and tends to favor the broadest possible interpretation of any contract between two Missouri citizens. The judge most likely to be assigned the case in Cole County plays poker with the lawyer who will represent the defendant. The judge most likely to be assigned the case in Camden County is known to be impartial and unbiased to the point of deserving sainthood. So, where should the prudent plaintiff file the breach of contract suit? The most favorable venue would be Camden County. The plaintiff should seek the defendant's permission for the case to be filed, heard and decided in Camden County.

An American citizen gullible to the point of needing a guardian no doubt assumes that all judges in all courts of law are honest, oozing integrity by being impartial, unbiased, and are thus above reproach. The sad truth is that judges are just human beings with strong opinions and bias that can be purchased by providing something the judge wants to the point of slobbering (such as a massive bribe). Judicial decisions at any level of our legal system from the municipal courts to the US Supreme Court can be purchased with political favoritism which promises rapid advances in the relevant judge's legal career (such as an appointment to the bench of a higher level court ---- like moving from the circuit level bench to the appellate court level).

Judges can also be bought by rich and well connected law firms with political clout which can affect the judge's legal career. US Supreme Court justices spend their entire tenure on the High Court engaged in partisan politics and repayment to those responsible for his/her Presidential appointment (see history of Elena Kagan).

Judges also tend to favor the lawyers who are constantly practicing law in the judge's courtroom. Most judges are very hostile toward individuals who represent themselves and thus do not enrich the legal fraternity.

Judges hide their bias, prejudice and purchased judicial decisions behind the fluid nature of the laws (which are hotly debated in the appellate courts). Judges also hide their biased and/or bought decisions by handing down opinions that are contrary to the factual evidence submitted but quote reams of similar cases supporting the judge's misrepresentation of the facts submitted to the court. In other words, the facts paint one picture but the judge flips the canvas over and paints a factual scenario that supports the judge's biased and/or purchased ruling. Judges can get by with such chicanery because the appellate courts do not decide issues of fact but rather issues of law (did the judge's ruling comply with established law when applying the applicable law to the facts painted by the judge).

Appellate court judges use the same level of judicial dishonesty when handing down appellate decisions that favor special interest entities; political cronies; rich, well connected law firms; and rich parties paying bribes. The appellate courts hide their judicial malfeasance by issuing rulings without an explanation as to how the appellate judges arrived at the decisions. The appellate decision will be one line which says something like "the trial court is affirmed," or "the appeal is denied." By handing down such one line opinions, law school students reading the trial court and appellate court case history are unaware that the appellate judges denied or granted the appeals without any legal justification for the decisions.

In other words, the appellate courts hand down decisions that are based only on what the appellate judges want without regard to what established law actually demands. It is a common practice for the appellate courts to hand down decisions to accommodate the legal fraternity, and especially so if the appealing individual is not represented by a member of the fraternity. The US Supreme Court can refuse to hear any particular case at the sole discretion of the nine justices. One way to be sure that the nine wise ones will not hear the case is to allege malfeasance or corruption within the lower courts which were involved with the case history.

These are indeed very serious charges about which neither the news media, prosecutors nor politicians get very excited because the legal fraternity is so transparent and long standing. One way to destroy your journalistic, political or legal career is to challenge the legal fraternity which reigns from the municipal court level to the United States Supreme Court. Such being the case, how does the American public composed primarily of individuals with no education above high school cope with such entrenched total power? The only answer is the pig trucks just like the Ghanians discovered when they loaded up the political pigs, drove them into a deserted area, shot them dead and buried them in crude and unmarked mass graves. Perhaps the night of the pig hunters is closer than the pigs believe.

The Medtronic Sprint Fidelis Multi-district Litigation (MDL 08-1905) is an excellent example as to why the pig trucks may be the only solution to the absolute corruption of America's legal system. The first product liability cases charging Medtronic with killing over a dozen (more like five hundred) people and injuring tens of thousands were filed in courts across the United States in October 2007 and thereafter.

Medtronic is a manufacturer of medical devices and enjoys sales of twelve to fifteen billion. Medtronic's biggest money makers are pacemakers and implantable defibrillators. However Medtronic's defibrillators have been plagued with major quality problems from 2003 through 2007. The two most serious problems were CHI 4420L batteries and the Medtronic Sprint Fidelis defibrillator leads. The Chi 4420L batteries were prone to short-circuiting and depleting the battery charge. The Sprint Fidelis leads were prone to fracture at an unacceptable rate and trigger repetitive shocks causing cardiac injuries coupled with intense pain and suffering. Several people were killed when their Medtronic defibrillators fractured and tens of thousands more were injured.

During this same time window, the FDA was totally corrupted (see letter from nine FDA scientists to President Obama). The Medtronic defibrillators were being inspected every six years instead of the regulatory two years. The Sprint Fidelis Leads were only bench tested and were not evaluated as to durability in an implanted state. The super thin lead was an attempt to gain a larger market share with a lead easier to thread through cardiac veins and creating less obstruction of the critical pathway to the patient's heart.

Medtronic became aware of the shorting problem with the CHI 4420L batteries in 2003 but kept dumping the defective defibrillators into the stream of interstate commerce for another two years (see opinion by Federal Judge James Rosenbaum).

Medtronic became aware of the Sprint Fidelis unacceptable fracture rate in 2004 (shortly after introduction of the leads into interstate commerce). It soon became very obvious that the fracture rate was accelerating with elapsed time since implanting and thus should be removed from the market. However,

Medtronic continued to dump the defective defibrillators into the stream of interstate commerce until October 15, 2007 such that a total of roughly 268,000 individuals have been implanted with the killer defibrillators. The Sprint Fidelis fracture rate admitted by Medtronic during 2007 was pushing 3.0% and the anticipated fracture rate during the fourth and fifth years following implantation was calculated by medical researchers to approach 30.0%. The fracture rate during 2011 and into 2012 ranged from nine to twelve percent depending upon sex, age and physical exertion. Thus, in 2007 over 8,000 recipients of the Sprint Fidelis leads were expected to experience lead fracture and in early 2012 the number of individuals experiencing lead fracture was calculated at approximately 25,000.

Medtronic has warned more than 87,000 individuals that their defibrillators might malfunction. More than 20,000 individuals have undergone removal surgery with a high risk of sudden cardiac death. The cumulative unnecessary cost to Medicare and the taxpayers for the defective defibrillators and related medical expenses now stands at around one billion dollars. Medtronic has reaped roughly ten dollars in bottom line profits for every one dollar paid out in massive bribes and settlement of product liability law suits until Judge Richard Kyle slammed the door on Medtronic's liability for murdering perhaps five hundred people and seriously injuring 25,000 or so. It is quite possible the Kyle pocketed three to five million dollars of Medtronic's bribe money.

This ten to one return on bribe and settlement money probably gave Medtronic's accountants charged with risk analysis a prolonged orgasm. Oh hell, if a few thousand senior citizens got seriously injured and a few hundred died somewhat prematurely, what's the big deal? Those old folks were going to die anyway. Just think about all the good cardiac implants Medtronic can develop with the ten billion or so in profits contributed by seniors who are enduring pain and suffering and turning up their toes. Somebody's gotta pay for research!

Medtronic admits to thirteen people killed by their Medtronic defibrillator equipped with recalled Sprint Fidelis leads. The number is more likely around 500 dead and 100,000 injured. When an old fart implanted with a defibrillator dies suddenly for whatever reason considered "natural" the surviving family members don't rush out and pay for an autopsy to see if the deceased's defibrillator might have malfunctioned. Morticians and pathologists aren't generally overwhelmed with concern for the quality history of the deceased's defibrillator. Units returned to Medtronic for "sudden death analysis" are more than likely going to be rated as absolutely reliable beyond expectation or the unit and paperwork may get forever "lost."

A medical devices manufacturer paying out a hundred million or so in bribes and intentionally dumping defibrillators known to be defective, extremely dangerous and perhaps fatal into the stream of interstate commerce can certainly be depended upon to lose a few returns with accompanying paperwork and fudge the statistics a bit on adverse field reports.

Statistically speaking, if thirteen people died out of around 8,000 people injured, when the Sprint Fidelis fracture rate was three percent, then how many would be expected to die out of 25,000 while the fracture rate escalates to thirty percent?   And, suppose that the number of deaths out of 8,000 injured was actually 110 rather than thirteen; then, how many people did Medtronic murder?

By June, 2011 the number of product liability suits filed against Medtronic by those injured by Medtronic and survivors of those intentionally murdered by Medtronic for profit had climbed to around 10,000. The suits were filed in both state courts and federal courts across the United States. A provision exists under federal procedural law which permits a large number of cases filed against the same defendant to be consolidated before one federal judge for pre-trial motions and for discovery matters (interrogatories, requests for admissions, production of documents, depositions, affidavits, etc.). This is called multi-district litigation (MDL) and is limited to pre-trial motions and discovery. Thereafter, the cases are remanded back to the courts where the cases were originally filed. It is not the intent of MDL for a single federal judge to dismiss the consolidated cases. However, one type of pre-trial motion is a motion to dismiss the complaints because the relevant law does not provide a remedy for the damages complained of in the complaints (cases).

The "relevant law" is constantly changing as appellate courts and the US Supreme Court continue to hand down decisions that overturn existing laws. Thus, a motion to dismiss is a proper motion to file in a MDL court before a MDL judge (like Judge Richard Kyle). The MDL judge decides whether the existing and applicable laws do in fact provide a remedy for the damages complained of in the complaints. If not, the MDL judge has the judicial authority to dismiss the consolidated cases.

An individual plaintiff (person filing the complaint) can timely object to having his/her specific case transferred to an MDL court before an MDL judge on the legal grounds that the individual's complaint is not based upon the same legal theories of recovery of damages as the consolidated cases such that the pre-trial motions and discovery will be different from the other consolidated cases. The notice of objections is filed in the MDL court and decided by the US Judicial Panel On Multi-district Litigation. The panel is made up of federal judges from various federal judicial districts. The "panel" can affirm the transfer to the MDL court or remand the case back to the court where the case was originally filed.

Medtronic's lawyers (the finest that money can buy) pushed for consolidation of the Medtronic Sprint Fidelis Product Liability Litigation before Judge Kyle, a federal judge sitting on the bench in the US District Court for the District of Minnesota located in Minneapolis (MDL 08-1905, the Sprint Fidelis litigation). Why did Medtronic's lawyers want Judge

Kyle appointed as the MDL judge? Well, for starters, Judge Kyle's son works for and holds stock in a law firm that is directly involved in Medtronic's legal affairs. This is a serious conflict of interest which should have immediately disqualified Judge Kyle as a candidate to serve as the MDL judge presiding over MDL 08-1905. The "panel" in a transparent effort to accommodate some key figures in the above described legal fraternity appointed Judge Kyle anyway. Counsel representing the consolidated plaintiffs filed a motion to have Kyle disqualified based on a glaring conflict of interest. Kyle, of course denied the motion. Why? Perhaps a definite indication that he would be agreeable to a major bribe by Medtronic who had already been documented by the US Department of Justice as bribing physicians and other health care providers as well as ripping off Medicare thereby raiding the public treasury.

Judge Kyle remained the judge presiding over MDL 08-1905 and dismissed all the consolidated complaints on the basis that the relevant law does not provide a remedy for the damages complained of in the consolidated complaints. Isn't that interesting? Medtronic kills a bunch of seniors and injures tens of thousands more and such killings and injuries inflicted creates zero liability on the part of Medtronic. Wow! That ruling by Kyle should be worth a minimum of three to five million dollars from Medtronic's bribe budget.

What flash of judicial brilliance did Kyle rely upon to keep 10,000 or so seniors from recovering injuries inflicted by Medtronic defibrillators equipped with Sprint Fidelis leads (leads known for years to Medtronic, implanting physicians and hospitals to be potentially defective, extremely dangerous and fatal to a predictable percentage of seniors implanted with the deadly devices)??? Well, "federal preemption" sounded real good and could be wrapped in the theory of "more benefits than harm" to placate the general public.

Exactly what is federal preemption as judicially manipulated by Judge Kyle and what is it based upon? Well, federal preemption means that federal law overrides state law because the FDA pre-market approval is sufficient to safeguard the health and safety of the American people with respect to medical devices such as pacemakers and defibrillators. Therefore, the US Supreme Court in the case cited as Riegel v. Medtronic (detailed on pages 129-158) ruled that federal law preempts state law product liability suits when the state law contains requirements, specifications or regulations that are different from the requirements, specifications or regulations spelled out in the FDA pre-market approval for the medical device in question.

In other words, product liability suits against medical devices manufacturers based upon state laws that are the same as or simply parallel the FDA pre-market approval requirements, specifications or regulations are NOT preempted by federal law.

Judge Kyle manipulated the Riegel decision wording to slam the door on all Medtronic liability in connection with Sprint Fidelis leads by concluding that the FDA being totally corrupted (as reported by nine

FDA scientists to President Obama) was adequately protecting the American people from a medical devices manufacturer who has a long history of bribing physicians, hospitals and other health care providers while ripping off Medicare and intentionally dumping into the stream of interstate commerce deadly defibrillators know for years to Medtronic, implanting physicians and hospitals to be "killer defibrillators" while at the same time spending a hundred million dollars advertising the safety and reliability of those same defibrillators (see letter from Senator Charles Grassley to the CEO of Medtronic detailed at pages 93-94).

This rewriting by Judge Kyle of product liability laws in effect for a century or more is just the tip of the iceberg constituting an undeniable example of system-wide corruption which can perhaps be illuminated by one of Alexander's appeals now pending before the US Court of Appeals for the Eighth Judicial Circuit. Readers, please be patient. The next chapter contains a very simple step-by-step outline for filing suit against

Medtronic without incurring any up front legal fees for representation by an attorney. The language is not technical and is easy to follow).

CASE NUMBER: **12-1157**

IN THE UNITED STATES COURT OF APPEALS

FOR THE EIGHTH JUDICIAL CIRCUIT

DONALD K. ALEXANDER,

APPELLANT/PLAINTIFF,

V.

CH ALLIED SERVICES, INC (dba BOONE HOSPITAL CENTER), DANIEL ROTHERY, NANCY TUNE, MISSY ARNOLD, WILLIAM A. HAWKINS, SUSAN ALPERT, KATHLEEN ERICKSON DiGIORNO, STEPHEN N. OESTERLE, M.D., GARY ELLIS, AND MEDTRONIC, INCORPORATED, APPELLEES/DEFENDANTS.

ON APPEAL FROM THE U.S. DISTRICT COURT FOR

THE WESTERN DISTRICT OF MISSOURI

CENTRAL DIVISION

District Court case number 2:10 CV 04081 NKL

APPELLANT/PLAINTIFF'S REPLY BRIEF

DONALD K. ALEXANDER

31057 OAK RIDGE DRIVE

ROCKY MOUNT, MISSOURI 65072

(573) 557-2071 donalexander557@gmail.com

TABLE OF CONTENTS

SUMMARY OF THE CASE FROM REPLY BRIEF

PERSPECTIVE

Appellant/Plaintiff Donald K. Alexander

originally filed suit against Appellees/Defendants in the

US District Court for the Western District of Missouri,

Central Division. The complaint contained damage

allegations under both the Federal Civil RICO Statute

and under Missouri tort laws; and the allegations under

each legal theory of recovery were set apart within five

separate counts contained in the complaint. It was

necessary for Appellant/Plaintiff to set forth all his

damages under both Civil RICO and Missouri tort law

to avoid having the alleged state tort law damages

barred by *failure to consolidate all known and related*

damages claims against Defendants in the same civil

action.

The Civil RICO alleged damages were set forth in

Count One and the only damages claimed were property

and/or financial damages in the form of a fraudulently

advertised defibrillator sold to Appellant/Plaintiff by

Medtronic through a marketing arrangement with Boone

Hospital Center with foreknowledge on the part of both

Medtronic and Boone Hospital Center employees/agents

that said defibrillator was potentially defective,

extremely dangerous and perhaps fatal to Appellant/

Plaintiff. Said defibrillator was both sold to Appellant/

Plaintiff and billed through Boone Hospital Center and

included implantation within Boone Hospital Center by

the attending physician assisted by Boone Hospital

Center's employees/agents. The attending physician's

services were billed separately. As pointed out in

Appellant/ Plaintiff's original brief, the purchase and

implanting of said defibrillator is no different in terms

of buyer and seller than a purchase transaction involving

a gas fired furnace installed by an independent

contractor. Said defibrillator was, subsequent to actual

implantation, recalled by Medtronic but unfortunately

was permanently wired to Appellant/Plaintiff's heart

removing any doubt whatsoever that the implanted

cardiac device had become the personal property of

Appellant/Plaintiff. The debt incurred by Appellant/

Plaintiff for said defibrillator and "installation" was

measured in hard cash denomination and such money

was most definitely Appellant/Plaintiff's property such

that the fraud perpetrated upon Appellate/Plaintiff by

Medtronic, and Boone Hospital Center's

employees/agents acting in compliance therewith, most

definitely represented a property/financial loss to

Appellant/Plaintiff; and such damages are the sole

damages alleged by Appellant/ Plaintiff in Count One.

Count One also included numerous factual

allegations in support of Appellant/ Plaintiff's

contention that Medtronic's pattern of criminal behavior

and Boone Hospital Center's employees/agents'

foreknowledge thereof established Medtronic's liability

under Civil RICO, and Boone Hospital Center's

employees/agents as accomplices in the criminal

conspiracy being orchestrated by Medtronic. Such

factual allegations are jury issues and not to be decided

by opposing counsel.

Count Two set forth additional factual allegations

in support of damages claimed by Appellant under

RSMO Chapter 538 in connection with intentional

medical negligence on the part of Boone Hospital

Center's employees/agents pursuant to foreknowledge

that the Medtronic defibrillator they were selling to

Appellant/Plaintiff and helping to implant was known to

be potentially defective, extremely dangerous and

perhaps fatal to recipients thereof thereby breaching the

minimum standard of medical care required of hospital

employees/agents. Moreover, Appellant/Plaintiff had,

prior to implantation of said defibrillator, specifically

requested Boone Hospital Center's Admissions and

Information Registrar (Missy Arnold) to verify the

quality history of said Medtronic defibrillator about to

be wired to Appellant/Plaintiff's heart.

Count Two further alleged that Boone Hospital

Center has a fundamental duty to maintain quality

control procedures and reasonable safeguards to assure

that Medtronic defibrillators being inventoried, sold to,

and implanted into hospital patients by Boone Hospital

Center's employees/agents are not potentially defective,

extremely dangerous and perhaps fatal to recipients

thereof. Count Two sets forth numerous factual

allegations in support of the alleged foreknowledge of

Boone Hospital Center's employees/agents that

Medtronic has a history of dumping defective

defibrillators into the stream of interstate commerce in

such a flagrant manner that denial of said

foreknowledge by said employee/agents would be both

laughable and moronic. These factual allegations are

jury issues and not to be decided by opposing counsel.

Count Three sets forth damages alleged pursuant

to provisions of Title 18 USC Section 1962(d) [which

provides for attorneys' fees] and under RSMO 537.050

(In no case shall the right of action of any party injured

by the commission of any felony or misdemeanor be

deemed or adjudged to be merged into such felony or

misdemeanor; but he may recover the amount of

damages sustained thereby in an action to be brought

before any court or tribunal of competent jurisdiction).

Thus, under Count Three Appellant/Plaintiff claimed

attorney's fees provided by 18 USC Section 1962(d) and

actual, compensatory and punitive damages under

RSMO 537.050.

Count Four set forth damages alleged by

Appellant/Plaintiff pursuant to "employer vicarious

liability" for the tortious acts committed against

Appellant/Plaintiff by Medtronic's employee/agent,

Brian Rysdam, within Appellant/Plaintiff's operating

room at Boone Hospital Center (acting in furtherance of

the criminal conspiracy being orchestrated by

Medtronic). The liability of a corporation for the tortious

acts of its employees/agents carrying out the routine

business of the corporations is black letter law. The

factual allegations connected therewith are jury issues.

Count Five set forth damages alleged by

Appellant/Plaintiff for criminal false advertising and fraud on the part of Medtronic in flagrant violation of RSMO 407.020(1) and 407.020(2)&(3). Count Five alleges numerous factual issues in support of said false advertising and fraud which are in the province of the jury and not opposing counsel.

For opposing counsel to contend that Count One (the primary Civil RICO count) is a personal injury claim is akin to arguing that a gas fired furnace installed by an independent contractor which blows up and cripples the buyer does not represent a property or financial loss because the buyer was injured in the explosion. Such a contention is actually alleging black is white, up is down, and crooked is straight.

TABLE OF AUTHORITIES

Lexicon Inc. v. Milberg Weiss Bershad Hynes & Lerach

523 U.S. 26, 40,

118 S. Ct. 956, 964, 140 L.Ed. 2D 62 (1988)

In re Baseball Bat Antitrust Litig. 112 F.Supp.,

2d 1175 (JPML Aug. 2000)

In re Fedex Ground Package Sys., Inc.

Employment Practices Litig.,

WL 3239330 (N.D. Ind. Aug. 12, 2010)

Brengettcy v. Horton, 423 F.2d 674, 680 (7th Cir.

2005)

Ashcroft v. Iqbal, 129 S. Ct. 1937, 1949 (2009)

quoting Twobbly, 550 U.S. at 570

STATUTES

Title 18 USC Sections 1962 and 1964   (Federal Civil

RICO)

RSMO Chapter 538   Intentional medical negligence

(punitive damages allowed)

RSMO 407.020(1)-(3)   False advertising and fraud

(class D felony)

RSMO 537.050   Damages allowed pursuant to

criminal acts

<u>JURISDICTIONAL STATEMENT</u>

The Judiciary Act of 1891, the Evarts Act, and the

Judiciary Act of 1925 established the authority for the

United States Courts of Appeal sitting in nine judicial

circuits including the United States Court of Appeals for

the Eighth Judicial Circuit to hear and decide appeals

taken from the United States District Courts. Title 18

U.S.C. Section 1962 authorizes original jurisdiction in

the United States District Courts to preside over Civil

RICO cases brought pursuant to Title 18 U.S.C. Section

1962. Appellant/Plaintiff filed a Section 1962 Civil

RICO suit in the United States District Court for the

Western District of Missouri, Central Division. Said

District Court dismissed the suit December 19, 2011

(FINAL ORDER). Appellant/Plaintiff filed a notice of

Appeal to the United States Court of Appeals for the

Eighth Circuit on December 20, 2011. Said appeal was

docketed by the District Court accordingly.

PROCEDURAL HISTORY

Appellant/Plaintiff originally filed suit against

Medtronic in the US District Court for the District of

Minnesota based upon product liability theories of

recovery of damages. Subsequently, all such suits

against Medtronic were consolidated into an MDL

proceeding within said District Court before Judge

Richard H. Kyle presiding over the MDL litigation.

Anticipating the US Supreme Court decision in Riegel v.

Medtronic, Appellant/Plaintiff filed a voluntary

dismissal without prejudice in the MDL Court and filed

suit against Medtronic in the Morgan County, Missouri

Circuit Court alleging damages pursuant to criminal

false advertising proscribed by RSMO 407.020(1)-(3).

This state tort law case based upon criminal acts (which

cannot be authorized by FDA's PMA and therefore not

subject to federal preemption) was removed to the US

District Court sitting in Jefferson City, Missouri and

then transferred to Judge Kyle in said MDL Court.

Appellant/Plaintiff timely objected to said transfer based

on lack of subject matter jurisdiction but said state case

remained firmly and semi-permanently buried beneath

said product liability presided over by Judge Kyle in

Minneapolis (next door to Medtronic's world

headquarters). Judge Kyle denied Appellant/Plaintiff's

motions to remand to Missouri for lack of subject matter

jurisdiction.

Judge Kyle dismissed all product liability liability

cases included in the MDL Master Consolidated

Complaint on January 5, 2009 and ordered the other

Plaintiffs to show cause why their complaints should not

also be dismissed. Appellant/Plaintiff timely responded

to the "show cause order" on the basis that a suit

alleging criminal behavior (criminal false advertising

and fraud) is not a suit alleging product liability and

therefore the MDL Court lacked subject matter

jurisdiction. Judge Kyle never responded to

Appellant/Plaintiff's answer to the show cause order and

subsequently denied Appellant's motion to remand for

lack of subject matter jurisdiction without explanation.

On April 19, 2010 Appellant/Plaintiff filed a Civil

RICO suit in the US District Court sitting in Jefferson

City, Missouri pursuant to Title 18 USC 1962 and 1964.

After service upon all Defendants, over

Appellant/Plaintiff's timely objections alleging lack of

subject matter jurisdiction, this Civil RICO case was

also transferred to the MDL Court presided over by

Judge Kyle. Judge Kyle denied a timely filed motion to

remand.

Because medical research organizations were

predicting a Medtronic defibrillator Sprint Fidelis lead

fracture rate of 30% during the fourth year following

implantation, Appellant/Plaintiff opted into a global

settlement fund established by Medtronic in order to

obtain funds to have Appellant/Plaintiff's said Sprint

Fidelis lead surgically removed. Medtronic's

spokesperson, Christopher Garland announced that the

settlement fund was limited to roughly 8,100 claimants

and the average allocation to each claimant was

expected to be around $33,000. The Plaintiffs' Steering

Committee lawyers advised Appellant/Plaintiff that his

allocation from the fund might be around $75,000 and

that the allocation check should be available to cash in

July, 2011.

     After Appellant/plaintiff opted into the fund, the

fund was reduced by 48 million dollars and the number

of claimants was increased by 42%. Appellant/Plaintiff

was subsequently informed that his allocation check

would be $1,000 less a 40% holdback for Medicare

reimbursement and a 9% holdback for common benefits

attorneys' fees leaving a net allocation of approximately

$500; and that an additional allocation MIGHT be

available within a year or so to compensate Appellant

/Plaintiff for multiple inappropriate shocking episodes

and surgical removal of the Sprint Fidelis lead.

However, the amount of such additional allocation was

indefinite and the payout date was extremely tenative.

On September 22, 2011 Appellant/Plaintiff's said

Civil RICO suit was finally remanded back to Missouri

with respect to the non-Medtronic Defendants. On

October 11, 2011 Appellant/Plaintiff filed a FRCP Rule

60B(1)(3)(6) motion in said MDL Court to set aside the

voluntary dismissal order entered by Judge Kyle

pertaining to the Medtronic Defendants in

Appellant/Plaintiff's said Civil RICO suit remanded

back to Missouri. The grounds for said Rule 60B motion

pled by Appellant/Plaintiff were surprise, misrepresen-

tation, and granting of said motion in the interest of

justice and fair play. The MDL court clerk's office

refused to docket the motion on the basis of lack of

jurisdiction pursuant to remand back to Missouri

whereupon Appellant/Plaintiff refiled the motion in the

US District Court sitting in Jefferson City, Missouri.

On December 19, 2011 said District Court denied

said Rule 60B motion without prejudice and referred the

motion back to Judge Kyle. This jurisdictional quagmire

left Appellant/Plaintiff totally confused such that to be

procedurally safe Appellant/Plaintiff, based upon said

denial in Missouri, refiled said motion in the MDL

Court which the clerk agreed to docket. Appellant/

Plaintiff waited for the MDL Plaintiffs' Steering

Committee lawyers and Medtronic's lawyers to to

respond to the motion as ordered by Judge Kyle. Said

Steering Committee lawyers responded alleging that the

US Supreme Court has addressed MDL Court

jurisdiction pursuant to remand issue and ruled that such

jurisdiction does not exist and cannot be bootstrapped in

the transferee Court (*citing Lexicon Inc. v. Milberg*

Weiss Bershad Hynes & Lerach 523 U.S. 26, 40,

118 S. Ct. 956, 964, 140 L.Ed. 2D 62 (1988), In re

Baseball Bat Antitrust Litig. 112 F.Supp., 2d 1175

(JPML Aug. 2000), In re Fedex Ground Package Sys.,

Inc. Employment Practices Litig., WL 3239330 (N.D.

Ind. Aug. 12, 2010) Brengettcy v. Horton, 423 F.2d 674,

680 (7ᵗʰ Cir. 2005), and Ashcroft v. Iqbal, 129 S. Ct.

1937, 1949 (2009) quoting Twobbly, 550 U.S. at 570

CLARIFICATION OF THE ISSUES

This appeal raises three primary issues to be decided by the Eighth Circuit: Does an MDL Court presiding over consolidated product liability suits have subject matter jurisdiction over a Federal Civil RICO suit which pleads no product liability claims whatsoever? Is an MDL Court divested of all jurisdiction pursuant to remand of cases back to the Courts where the cases were originally filed? Does a $72,000+ cardiac device wired to an individual's heart represent that individual's property and does the indebtedness incurred by that individual represent a financial and/or property loss when said device turns out to defective, dangerous and life threatening?

APPELLANT/PLAINTIFF'S ARGUMENT

Constitutional, statutory, procedural and case law

does not permit transfer of a Federal Civil RICO suit to an MDL Court presiding over consolidated product liability suits. The US Supreme Court has held that an MDL transferee Court is divested of all jurisdiction upon remand back to the transferor Court. It is axiomatic that a cardiac device wired to an individual's heart is that individual's property and the $72,000+ billed for said cardiac device represents both a property and financial loss when said cardiac device turns out to be dangerous and life threatening.

CONCLUSION

Because of the jurisdictional confusion and the probable bias created thereby toward Appellant/ Plaintiff's FRCP Rule 60B(1)(3)(6) motion in the Courts below, Appellant/Plaintiff prays the Eighth Circuit

Judges to rule on said motion and then to issue whatever

remand orders are deemed appropriate should the Eighth

Circuit elect to rule upon and grant said motion.

APPELLANT/PLAINTIFF HEREBY WAIVES

ORAL ARGUMENT

CERTIFICATE OF COMPLIANCE

The undersigned Appellant/Plaintiff, Donald K.

Alexander, certifies that this reply brief complies with

FRAP Rule 28 and all sections thereof in that the brief

contains 2,595 words and 218 lines in proportionally

faced face using 14 point font.

Signature: //Donald K. Alexander,

Appellant/Plaintiff

CERTIFICATE OF NO TRANSCRIPT ORDERED

The undersigned Appellant/Plaintiff, Donald K.

Alexander, hereby certifies that no transcript will be

ordered and the necessary portions of the original papers

filed in the District Court are attached hereto.

Signature: //*Donald K. Alexander*

Respectfully submitted,

//*Donald K. Alexander, Appellant/Plaintiff*

Donald K. Alexander
31057 Oak Ridge Drive
Rocky Mount, Missouri 65072
(573) 557-2071 donalexander557@gmail.com

The preceding background and partial procedural history plus the following narrative details the astounding list of crimes committed by federal judges in connection with the Civil RICO suit against Medtronic filed by Don Alexander. A series of federal crimes are committed when federal judges under color of law intentionally deprive a US citizen of civil rights guaranteed within the US Constitution. When multiple judges are involved, the criminal acts constitute a criminal conspiracy under color of law to deprive a US citizen of his/her civil rights for which the penalty is up to ten years in a federal prison.

Judge Richard H. Kyle, Judge Nanette K. Laughrey, Judge Kathryn H. Vratil, Judge Barbara S. Jones, Judge Majorie O. Rendell, Judge W. Royal Ferguson, Jr, Judge Paul J. Barbadoro and Judge Charles R. Breyer are not stupid nor incompetent federal judges. Each of these co-conspirators knew precisely what was going down in order to protect Medtronic, Incorporated from major civil liability and very probable criminal indictments of Medtronic's senior management team in connection with Alexander's said Civil RICO suit.

Why would eight federal judges risk their legal careers and possible imprisonment to stall, bury and desperately try to kill Alexander's said suit? The first and most probable reason is money and lots of it. It was common knowledge in 2010 that Medtronic had passed out tens of millions in illegal bribes to conceal the evidence that Medtronic had murdered a bunch of folks and intentionally injured tens of thousands more. A judicial decision to protect Medtronic was worth three to five million. Another reason is that all eight judges are prominent members of a legal fraternity that works together to benefit the fraternity rather than the politically unconnected. Medtronic hired some of the richest and most politically connected lawyers to hide Medtronic's crimes. Another reason is that both Medtronic (a multi-billion dollar corporation) and Medtronic's rich, politically connected law firms can exert tremendous influence as to which federal district judges move up to appellate judges and perhaps even a seat on the US Supreme Court. And, there is the "God Complex" and unrestrained egomania that permeates the federal bench.

Is this spiteful rambling or documented facts? Well, stay tuned, folks, because the documented facts are truly beyond belief. To examine the chronological conspiratorial acts, consider that Judge Kyle dismissed the consolidated Medtronic Sprint Fidelis Lead Litigation (MDL 08-1905) on January 5, 2009 (see relevant legal files which are public information). That MDL decision was appealed by lawyers for roughly 10,000 plaintiffs. The appellate decision was placed on hold when Medtronic's lawyers came up with a clever scheme to offer a global settlement fund that would basically rip off the plaintiffs and enrich the lawyers representing the plaintiffs by approximately 107 million dollars while at the same time using fund money to reimburse Medicare for a hundred million or so of the money paid out of the public treasury (around one billion) for the false claims submitted to Medicare by Medtronic involving Medtronic's Sprint Fidelis leads.

The lawyers getting the 107 million warned the plaintiffs that their cases would be preempted by federal law so they best take whatever Medtronic was willing to shell out to compensate them for wrongful deaths and personal injuries (generally one thirty-third of what they had been led to believe they would receive). [See details at pages 41-46]. Alexander was promised up to $75,000 and later offered a check for $500 which he declined to accept.

The settlement scam was a transparent scheme between Medtronic's lawyers and the plaintiffs' lawyers to protect Medtronic and rip off the plaintiffs. However, this scam is minor compared to the conspiratorial acts committed by the aforementioned eight federal judges. Judge Kyle dismissed the consolidated product liability suits on January 5, 2009. Alexander filed the Civil Rico suit against Medtronic on April 19, 2010 (one year and three months AFTER Judge Kyle ordered dismissal of the consolidated product liability suits. There is zero commonality between product liability suits and a Civil RICO suit. There is not a scintilla of statutory, case or procedure law that would permit a Civil RICO suit to be buried in a MDL court beneath dismissed consolidated product liability suits. The only possible purpose behind doing so would be to delay, continuously stall and hopefully kill the Civil RICO suit. But, that is precisely what Judge Laughrey did. She sent the suit to Judge Kyle to be buried beneath the dismissed consolidated product liability suits on August 23, 2010.

The six panel judges ignored Alexander's timely filed objections to accommodate Judges Kyle and Laughrey. Alexander filed several timely motions to remand to Laughrey's court in Missouri from Kyle's court in Minneapolis. Kyle summarily denied the motions. Why? He wanted to delay, stall and perhaps find some less obvious way to kill Alexander's suit.

However, Alexander filed complaints against Kyle with the Eighth Circuit Court of Appeals and with the US Supreme Court Justice Samuel Alito who has oversight responsibility for the Eighth Circuit. The complaints were essentially ignored but made Kyle somewhat uneasy. Finally, on September 22, 2011, Kyle remanded Alexander's Civil RICO suit back to Judge Laughrey. Judge Laughrey fiddled with the suit for a couple more months and then dismissed it one year and five months after Alexander filed the Civil RICO suit in Laughrey's court in Jefferson City, Missouri. During the seventeen months,   Alexander was not permitted by either Kyle of Laughrey to conduct discovery nor issue any subpoenas.

What was the legal basis upon which Laughrey dismissed Alexander's Civil RICO suit after seventeen months of languishing beneath totally unrelated litigation??   Judge Laughrey actually ruled that the $72,000 billed to Alexander for the defective Medtronic defibrillator wired to his heart did not represent either a property nor financial loss!!!

CHAPTER FIVE

A complete guide and required documents to sue
Medtronic for damages in your county circuit court

Alexander's appeals continue to languish before
the US Court of Appeals for the Eighth Judicial Circuit.
Perhaps the appellate judges will find time to issue a
ruling during the 21st century. In any event it appears
that the federal judges are going to do whatever it takes
to absolve Medtronic of all liability in connection with
the senior citizens killed and injured.

Therefore, it is not prudent to file any claim
against Medtronic within the federal court system. It is
possible to sue Medtronic for criminal bribery, criminal
conspiracies and criminal fraud within the County
Circuit Courts scattered across the United States
(carefully read the author's foreword to understand why
the county suits are possible). If you, the reader, wish to

file a state county suit against Medtronic, simply follow the step-step outline presented below:

Step one: If you have been injured or terrorized by a potentially defective Medtronic defibrillator implanted into your chest and wish to file suit against Medtronic for damages suffered by you pursuant to criminal acts committed by Medtronic's management team, look up the telephone number for the State Court sitting in the city or county where you reside. Call the clerk's office and get the mailing address for the court and the filing fee for three defendants (Medtronic and the physician plus the hospital that implanted your Medtronic defibrillator). Obtain the mailing address and telephone number for the physician and hospital that implanted your defibrillator. Write down the exact nature of the damages which you are claiming (see page entitled "Why Sue Medtronic" at website medtronic murders.com for possible damages you can consider).

Step two: Use the sample suits shown below. You can edit the damages claimed and claim more or less damages as you see fit (see the website page entitled "Why Sue Medtronic" to select your damages). Remember, at trial your attorney will have to prove up the damages you claim in the form of actual or compensatory damages. If you are unsure, use the damages wording and amounts that appear in the sample complaint. Your finished complaint should look like the example below with your personal information and court caption substituted for Don Alexander's personal data.

IN THE CIRCUIT COURT

FOR

MORGAN COUNTY, MISSOURI

CASE NO: (to be assigned)

DONALD K. ALEXANDER,   )

   Plaintiff,   )

VS.   )

MEDTRONIC, INCORPORATED, AND   )

CH ALLIED HEALTH SERVICES, INC.   )

(dba as "Boone Hospital Center)   )

Defendants.   )

PETITION FOR PECUNIARY AND PERSONAL INJURY DAMAGES PURSUANT TO CRIMINAL CONSPIRACY, BRIBERY, AND CONSUMER FRAUD

This is a civil action to recover pecuniary and

personal injury damages pursuant to felonious criminal

acts committed by Defendants named herein against

Plaintiff Donald K. Alexander. The US Department of

Justice announcements are quoted only to show that the

criminal acts complained of by Plaintiff are well

documented and do relate to when such criminal acts became public knowledge. Therefore, this civil action is not filed under any Federal law or Federal statute but rather under state intentional tort law pursuant to criminal acts which damaged Plaintiff herein. Said criminal acts involved criminal conspiracies, criminal bribery, and intentional consumer fraud which directly and proximately inflicted upon Plaintiff pecuniary and personal injury damages more fully described herein. Plaintiff Alexander (hereinafter "Alexander") appears as Plaintiff Pro Se.

1.

JURISDICTION AND VENUE.

Plaintiff Alexander is a citizen of Missouri who resides in Morgan County, Missouri at 31057 Oak Ridge Drive, Rocky Mount, Missouri 65072. He is above the

age of majority for the State of Missouri, retired, and
was knowingly, intentionally, and fraudulently sold on
July 6, 2007 a defective Medtronic defibrillator by
Boone Hospital employees/agents pursuant to the
recommendation of Dr. Dan Pierce and Boone Hospital
staff whereby Alexander suffered financial and
personal injury damages. CH Allied Services, Inc. [dba
as Boone Hospital Center] (hereinafter "Boone
Hospital") operates a medical center located at 1600
East Broadway, Columbia, Missouri 65201. Alexander
suffered his injuries in Morgan County, Missouri
pursuant to Boone Hospitals' complicity in the criminal
bribing of physicians by Medtronic, Incorporated
(hereinafter "Medtronic"). Medtronic does business in
all fifty states and around the world. Therefore,
jurisdiction and venue are proper in the Circuit Court for
Morgan County, Missouri. The amount in controversy
(actual damages in excess of $103,000.00) is well above
the threshold dollar value required for docketing in the
Morgan County Circuit Court (not including

compensatory and punitive damages).

2.

STATUTE OF LIMITATIONS

On December 12, 2011 the statute of limitations time window pertaining to this suit was opened by the United States Department of Justice (hereinafter USDOJ) which issued the following press release: *"On December 12, the US Department of Justice announced yet another victory in the war against healthcare fraud. Medtronic Inc., the world's largest maker of medical devices, has agreed to pay a 23.5 million dollar settlement to the US government to settle a lawsuit alleging that the company violated the False Claims Act. According to the allegations, Medtronic paid between $1,000 and $2,000 to physicians in order to persuade them to implant the company's pacemakers and defibrillators – rather than competitors' devices – into Medicare and Medicaid patients. The Government accused Medtronic of submitting false claims to*

Medicare and Medicaid by offering doctors these kickbacks under the guise of post-market studies and device registries.

3.

The foregoing USDOJ December 12, 2011 announcement disclosing the criminal bribing of physicians pursuant to multiple criminal conspiracies involving Medtronic and implanting physicians plus the criminal defrauding of Medtronic defibrillator and pacemaker recipients provided Alexander for the first time with information and evidence sufficient to establish standing to sue Medtronic for financial and personal injury damages directly attributable to said criminal bribery, criminal conspiracy and criminal fraud. The mutual bribery agreement and cooperation between Medtronic and bribed physicians to withhold critical defective product information from potential recipients in exchange for the bribe payments to physicians constitutes a felonious criminal conspiracy.

The USDOJ had issued prior press releases involving investigations of Medtronic for bribing physicians and hospitals to overcharge Medicare for unnecessary patient hospital confinement in connection with in-patient treatment with Medtronic's spinal fusion kits which require a simple outpatient procedure; and for bribery of physicians to promote Medtronic medical devices within the medical community (other physicians and health care providers). However, the USDOJ made public for the first time on December 12, 2011 the allegations that Medtronic has heavily bribed physicians to recommend to and implant into their heart patients suffering with deadly arrhythmias Medtronic defibrillators which both Medtronic and the implanting physicians knew or should have known (per FDA MAUDE data base) were potentially defective, extremely dangerous and fatal to a predictable percentage of individuals implanted with the killer defibrillators

4.

Medtronic, Dr. Dan Pierce and Boone Hospital

acting through each co-conspirator's employees/agents

withheld and concealed from Alexander the dangerous

and perhaps fatal nature of said defibrillator selected by

Dr. Pierce and approved by Boone Hospital's quality

assurance personnel. Boone Hospital's employees/agents

sold said defibrillator to Alexander and represented it to

be of the highest quality. Said defibrillator was pulled

from Boone Hospital's inventory, implanted into

Alexander with the aid and assistance of Boone Hospital

employees/agents, and subsequently billed to Alexander

by Boone Hospital along with the medical services to

implant the deadly cardiac device (billing in excess of

$72,000.00) An employee/agent of Medtronic (Brian

Rysdam) also directly assisted Dr. Dan Pierce with

Alexander's July 6-7, 2007 implantation with said

deadly Medtronic defibrillator. Thus, a defective and

dangerous dual chamber Medtronic pacemaker and

defibrillator known to Dr. Pierce, Boone Hospital and

Medtronic's employees and agents to be defective,

dangerous and perhaps fatal, was sold under false

pretenses to Plaintiff by Boone Hospital on July 6, 2007
and implanted into Plaintiff with the direct assistance of
a Medtronic employee/agent working alongside Dr.
Pierce and Boone Hospital employees/agents.

5.

Unknown to Alexander but well known within the
medical community recommending, selling and
implanting defibrillators on July 6, 2007, the day of
Alexander's implantation with said defective Medtronic
defibrillator, Public records (FDA MAUDE data base);
studies conducted by health care providers (such as
Minneapolis Heart Institute); medicals journals (such as
Heart Rhythm publications); doctors (such as Dr.
Sidney Wolfe and Dr. Robert Hauser); and watchdog
organizations (such as Public Citizen) had been warning
health care providers for six months prior to July 6,
2007 that the type of Medtronic defibrillator Alexander
was being implanted with is faulty, dangerous, and
unnecessarily and repeatedly shocking and injuring
heart patients implanted therewith such that numerous

patient deaths were plainly foreseeable. Dr. Robert

Hauser at the Minneapolis Heart Institute conducted

studies on said defective Medtronic defibrillators , and

both published his findings in HEART RHYTHM

Medical Journal (in March 2007) and warned

Medtronic as well as the FDA (in February 2007) that

the defibrillators were potentially defective, dangerous,

and should be removed from the market. Alexander's

Medtronic defibrillator malfunctioned twice and sent

him to emergency rooms at Lake Regional Hospital by

ambulance after which he was admitted to Lake

Regional Hospital intensive care units.

6.

Medtronic was cited by Federal Judge James

Rosenbaum for dumping tens of thousands of

defibrillators know to Medtronic management to be

defective and possibly fatal into the stream of interstate

commerce between March 2003 and February 2005.

Medtronic had, according to Judge Rosenbaum,

withheld   critical   defective   Medtronic   product

information during 2003 from both FDA and the general public when applying for pre-market approval (intentional perjury) to place a battery known to be defective and perhaps fatal into new cardiac implant models being introduced into the stream of interstate commerce. Moreover, Medtronic had, according to US Senator Charles Grassley, between January 2007 and October 15, 2007 intentionally dumped defibrillators known to Medtronic management to be potentially defective and possibly fatal to recipients thereof into the stream of interstate commerce. Consequently, it is quite obvious that Medtronic has adopted a pattern of criminal behavior as its routine method of conducting corporate business affairs.

7.

The US Department of Justice had prior to January, 2007 investigated Medtronic for paying bribes to health care providers and conspiring with hospitals to overcharge their patients for Medtronic's spinal fusion kits and related medical services. Although this criminal behavior on the part of Medtronic and the complicity of hospitals and physicians was not known to Plaintiff herein in July 2007, Medtronic's pattern of criminal behavior involving bribery and concealment of defective medical products was common knowledge within the medical community; especially those health care providers (including Boone Hospital) inventorying, selling and implanting Medtronic defibrillators. For Boone Hospital employees/agents directly involved in inventorying, selling, implanting and billing Medtronic defibrillators to claim ignorance of the quality history of Medtronic defibrillators is akin to denying that they are employed by Boone Hospital. In any event, there is certainly reasonable grounds for a jury to find that Boone Hospital employees/agents were in fact aware of Medtronic's pattern of criminal behavior and were complicit in the scamming of heart patients in need of an implantable defibrillator. Such complicity makes Boone Hospital employees involved with such intentional scamming co-conspirators by acting in furtherance of the criminal conspiracy being perpetrated by Medtronic (acting through its employees/agents).

8.

Upon information and belief, Medtronic acted through its senior management staff members and other employees/agents to bribe physicians to recommend and implant Medtronic defibrillators and pacemakers rather than competitive cardiac implants manufactured by other business entities. Medtronic concealed the defective nature of its defective defibrillators from potential recipients thereof and conspired with physicians and hospitals to scam recipients of Medtronic defibrillators. By dumping defective defibrillator inventories into an unsuspecting market rather than scrap the defective inventory, Medtronic reaped billions in pre-tax profits. Health care providers (like Boone Hospital) have benefited by the lucrative mark-up on Medtronic defibrillators plus over $30,000.00 in medical services billing for implantation of each of the defective devices.

9.

Although Plaintiff herein is not suing Medtronic under "product liability" theories of recovery of damages or for damages in connection with violation of the Federal Anti-kickback Statute or for massive ripoffs of Medicare and Medicaid, Medtonic has demonstrated a history of conspiring with both hospitals and physicians to rip off Medicare and Medicaid (see USDOJ investigation, findings and press release pertaining to Medtronic's spinal fusion kits). Medtronic further has a history of concealing adverse product information from recipients of its cardiac implants, from the FDA and Medicare/Medicaid. Medtronic dumped defective defibrillators containing batteries that were subject to short-circuiting into an unsuspecting market for two years (2003-2005) as cited by Federal Judge James Rosenbaum. Judge Rosenbaum also cited Medtronic for withholding said defective battery information from the FDA in order to equip new defibrillator models with the same type defective batteries (perjury). Senator Charles Grassley charged

Medtronic in October 2007 with criminal false advertising by launching in January 2007 a 100 million dollars mass media advertising campaign directed at potential recipients of implantable cardiac devices long after Medtronic management knew that the advertised cardiac devices were potentially defective and perhaps fatal.

10.

Medtronic has thus far escaped criminal indictments by paying a hundred and fifty million or so to the USDOJ to call off investigations thereby protecting complicit physicians and hospitals. Medtronic has reaped billions in profits for defective inventories while paying out a few hundred million in USDOJ settlements and settlement of civil suits. Nevertheless, Plaintiff herein had no standing to sue Medtronic due to Federal Preemption of product liability suits and lack of incriminating evidence to bring suits based upon criminal acts until the USDOJ on December 12, 2011 announced a settlement with Medtronic in connection with bribing physicians to the tune of $1,000.00 to

$2,000.00 for every Medtronic defibrillator which they recommended and implanted. Hospital staff knowingly acted in furtherance of the conspiracy orchestrated by Medtronic by going along with the defrauding of heart patients needing an implanted defibrillator/pacemaker in order to to reap the tidy mark-up plus major billings for related medical services which in fact constitutes a criminal conspiracy.

11.

Said criminal conspiracies have been directly responsible for Alexander being knowingly and intentionally subjected to sub-standard medical care, breach of trust, and breach of duties to render an acceptable level of medical care established by the medical profession and governing medical boards. Said conspiracies seriously interfered with the physician/patient relationship by substituting fraud and bribery for physician integrity, trust and independent medical judgment. Alexander has suffered both personal injuries and financial damages (see prayer for relief) in connection with said criminal fraud and criminal bribery reinforced by physicians' recommendations (based upon said criminal bribery) which Alexander relied on to his detriment. But for said pattern of criminal behavior orchestrated by Medtronic and the participation of physicians and hospitals in the criminal conspiracies perpetrated by Medtronic, Alexander would not have suffered pecuniary and personal injury damages (see prayer for relief).

PRAYER FOR RELIEF

Wherefore, Alexander respectfully prays this Honorable Court for judgment against Medtronic, and for an award to Alexander of actual financial damages in the amount of $73,000.00 (seventy-three thousand dollars ---- approximate dollar amount billed to Alexander for defective defibrillator and implanting); and for an award to Alexander of compensatory damages in an amount to be determined by the trier of facts to compensate for anxiety and depression, mental terror, sleeplessness, loss of consortium, future medical expenses and cardiac damage.

In addition, because Medtronic management inflicted said damages knowingly, intentionally, recklessly, and without regard for human life thereby demonstrating a depraved mindset,   Alexander further prays this Honorable Court for an award of punitive damages to Alexander   in an amount reasonably proportional to Medtronic's net worth and in an amount sufficient to dissuade others similarly situated from like conduct.

In addition, Alexander prays this Honorable Court for judgment against Boone Hospital in the amount of $31,000.00 (thirty-one thousand dollars) for surgical explanting of his defective Medtronic defibrillator.   In addition, Alexander prays this Honorable Court for an award to be paid by Boone Hospital of compensatory damages in an amount to be determined by the trier of facts.   Because Boone Hospital   through its employees/agents knowingly acted in furtherance of the criminal conspiracy perpetuated by Medtronic as described herein, Alexander further prays this Honorable Court for an award to Alexander of punitive damages to be paid by Boone Hospital in an amount to be determined by the trier of facts to dissuade others similarly situated from like conduct.

<u>Alexander hereby requests a jury trial.</u>

Respectfully submitted,

//Donald K. Alexander

31057 Oak Ridge Drive
Rocky Mount, Missouri 65072
(573) 557-2071
<u>donalexander557@gmail.com</u>

Second Sample <u>Edited Suit</u>

For the sake of possible confusion reduction, suppose that Phillip J. Adams is the individual who wants to file the suit against Medtronic in the local Circuit Court. Mr. Adams lives at 3515 Colorado Avenue in Eldon, Missouri 65026. Eldon, Missouri is located in Miller County and the county seat where the

Circuit Court is located is in Tuscumbia, Missouri 65082 Phillip's telephone number is (573) 392-1938 and his email address is philjulieadams@gmail.com. Adams was implanted at Lakewood Hospital located at 5685 Highway 54 in Osage Beach, Missouri 65065 on April 15, 2007 by Dr. John R. Smith.

The edited sample suit for Mr. Adams would look like the below suit:

IN THE CIRCUIT COURT

FOR

MILLER COUNTY, MISSOURI

CASE NO: (to be assigned)

PHILLIP J. ADAMS,   )

    Plaintiff,   )

MEDTRONIC, INCORPORATED, AND   )

LAKEWOOD HOSPITAL   )

    Defendants.   )

PETITION FOR PECUNIARY AND PERSONAL INJURY DAMAGES PURSUANT TO CRIMINAL CONSPIRACY, BRIBERY, AND CONSUMER FRAUD

This is a civil action to recover pecuniary and personal injury damages pursuant to felonious criminal acts committed by Defendants named herein against Plaintiff Phillip J. Adams. The US Department of Justice announcements are quoted only to show that the criminal acts complained of by Plaintiff are well documented and do relate to when said criminal acts became public knowledge. Therefore, this civil action is not filed under any Federal law or Federal statute but rather under state intentional tort law pursuant to criminal acts which damaged Plaintiff herein. Said criminal acts involved criminal conspiracies, criminal bribery, and intentional consumer fraud which directly and proximately inflicted upon Plaintiff pecuniary and

personal injury damages more fully described herein.

Plaintiff Phillip J. Adams (hereinafter "Adams")

appears as Plaintiff Pro Se.

1.

JURISDICTION AND VENUE.

Plaintiff Adams is a citizen of Missouri who resides in Miller County, Missouri at 3515 Colorado Avenue, Eldon, Missouri 65026. He is above the age of majority for the State of Missouri, retired, and was knowingly, intentionally, and fraudulently sold on April 15, 2007 a defective Medtronic defibrillator by Lakewood Hospital employees/agents pursuant to the recommendation of Dr. John R. Smith and Lakewood Hospital staff whereby Adams suffered financial and personal injury damages. Lakewood Hospital is located at 5685 Highway 54, Osage Beach, Missouri 65065. Adams suffered his injuries (defective defibrillator malfunctioning) in Miller County, Missouri pursuant to Lakewood Hospitals' complicity in the criminal bribing of physicians by Medtronic, Incorporated (hereinafter "Medtronic"). Medtronic does business in all fifty states and around the world. Therefore, jurisdiction and venue are proper in the Circuit Court for Miller County, Missouri. The amount in controversy (actual damages in excess of $103,000.00) is well above the threshold dollar value required for docketing in the Miller County Circuit Court (not including compensatory and punitive damages).

2.

STATUTE OF LIMITATIONS

On December 12, 2011 the statute of limitations time window pertaining to this suit was opened by the United States Department of Justice (hereinafter USDOJ) which issued the following press release: *"On December 12, the US Department of Justice announced yet another victory in the war against healthcare fraud.*

Medtronic Inc., the world's largest maker of medical devices, has agreed to pay a 23.5 million dollar settlement to the US government to settle a lawsuit alleging that the company violated the False Claims Act. According to the allegations, Medtronic paid between $1,000 and $2,000 to physicians in order to persuade them to implant the company's pacemakers and defibrillators – rather than competitors' devices – into Medicare and Medicaid patients. The Government accused Medtronic of submitting false claims to Medicare and Medicaid by offering doctors these kickbacks under the guise of post-market studies and device registries.

3.

The foregoing USDOJ December 12, 2011 announcement disclosing the criminal bribing of physicians pursuant to multiple criminal conspiracies involving Medtronic and implanting physicians plus the criminal defrauding of Medtronic defibrillator and pacemaker recipients provided Adams for the first time with   information and evidence sufficient to establish standing to sue Medtronic for financial and personal injury damages directly attributable to said criminal bribery, criminal conspiracy and criminal fraud. The mutual bribery agreement and cooperation between Medtronic and bribed physicians to withhold critical defective product information from potential recipients in exchange for the bribe payments to physicians constitutes a felonious criminal conspiracy. The USDOJ had issued prior press releases involving investigations of Medtronic for bribing physicians and hospitals to overcharge Medicare for unnecessary patient hospital confinement in connection with in patient treatment with Medtronic's spinal fusion kits which require a simple outpatient procedure; and for bribery of physicians to promote Medtronic medical devices within the medical community (other physicians and health care providers). However, the USDOJ made public for the first time on December 12, 2011 the allegations that Medtronic has heavily bribed physicians to recommend to and implant into their heart patients suffering with deadly arrhythmias Medtronic defibrillators which both Medtronic and the implanting physicians knew or should have known (per FDA MAUDE data base) were potentially defective, extremely dangerous and fatal to a predictable percentage of individuals implanted with the killer defibrillators.

4.

Medtronic, Dr. John R. Smith and Lakewood Hospital acting through each co-conspirator's employees/agents withheld and concealed from Adams the dangerous and perhaps fatal nature of said defibrillator selected by Dr. Smith and approved by Lakewood Hospital's quality assurance personnel. Lakewood Hospital's employees/agents sold said defibrillator to Adams and represented it to be of the highest quality. Said defibrillator was pulled from Lakewood Hospital's inventory, implanted into Adams with the aid and assistance of Lakewood Hospital's employees/agents, and subsequently billed to Adams by Lakewood Hospital along with the medical services to implant the deadly cardiac device (billing in excess of $72,000.00) An employee/agent of Medtronic also directly assisted Dr. Smith with Adams' April 15, 2007 implantation with said deadly Medtronic defibrillator. Thus, a defective and dangerous dual chamber Medtronic pacemaker and defibrillator known to Dr. Smith, Lakewood Hospital and Medtronic's employees and agents to be defective, dangerous and perhaps fatal, was sold under false pretenses to Adams by Lakewood Hospital on April 15, 2007 and implanted into Adams with the direct assistance of a Medtronic employee/ agent working alongside Dr. Smith and Lakewood Hospital employees/agents.

5.

Unknown to Adams but well known within the medical community recommending, selling and implanting defibrillators on April 15, 2007, the day of Adam's implantation with said defective Medtronic defibrillator, Public records (FDA MAUDE data base); studies conducted by health care providers (such as

Minneapolis Heart Institute); medicals journals (such as Heart Rhythm publications); doctors (such as Dr. Sidney Wolfe and Dr. Robert Hauser); and watchdog organizations (such as Public Citizen) had been warning health care providers for six months prior to July 6, 2007 that the type of Medtronic defibrillator Adams was being implanted with is faulty, dangerous, and unnecessarily and repeatedly shocking and injuring heart patients implanted therewith such that numerous patient deaths were plainly foreseeable. Dr. Robert Hauser at the Minneapolis Heart Institute conducted studies on said defective Medtronic defibrillators , and both published his findings in HEART RHYTHM Medical Journal (in March 2007) and warned Medtronic as well as the FDA (in February 2007) that the defibrillators were potentially defective, dangerous, and should be removed from the market. Adam's Medtronic defibrillator malfunctioned twice and sent him to emergency rooms at Lakewood Hospital by ambulance after which he was admitted to Lakewood

Hospital intensive care units.

6.

Medtronic was cited by Federal Judge James Rosenbaum for dumping tens of thousands of defibrillators know to Medtronic management to be defective and possibly fatal into the stream of interstate commerce between March 2003 and February 2005. Medtronic had, according to Judge Rosenbaum, withheld critical defective Medtronic product information during 2003 from both FDA and the general public when applying for pre-market approval (intentional perjury) to place a battery known to be defective and perhaps fatal into new cardiac implant models being introduced into the stream of interstate commerce. Moreover, Medtronic had, according to US Senator Charles Grassley, between January 2007 and October 15, 2007 intentionally dumped defibrillators known to Medtronic management to be potentially defective and possibly fatal to recipients thereof into the stream of interstate commerce. Consequently, it is quite obvious that Medtronic has adopted a pattern of criminal behavior as its routine method of conducting corporate business affairs.

7.

The US Department of Justice had prior to January, 2007 investigated Medtronic for paying bribes to health care providers and conspiring with hospitals to overcharge their patients for Medtronic's spinal fusion kits and related medical services. Although this criminal behavior on the part of Medtronic and the complicity of hospitals and physicians was not known to Adams in April 2007, Medtronic's pattern of criminal behavior involving bribery and concealment of defective medical products was common knowledge within the medical community; especially those health care providers (including Lakewood Hospital) inventorying, selling and implanting Medtronic defibrillators. For Lakewood Hospital employees/agents directly involved in inventorying, selling, implanting and billing Medtronic defibrillators to claim ignorance of the quality history of

Medtronic defibrillators is akin to denying that they are employed by Lakewood Hospital. In any event, there is certainly reasonable grounds for a jury to find that Lakewood Hospital employees/agents were in fact aware of Medtronic's pattern of criminal behavior and were complicit in the scamming of heart patients in need of an implantable defibrillator. Such complicity makes Lakewood Hospital employees involved with such intentional scamming co-conspirators by acting in furtherance of the criminal conspiracy being perpetrated by Medtronic (acting through its employees/agents).

8.

Upon information and belief, Medtronic acted through its senior management staff members and other employees/agents to bribe physicians to recommend and implant Medtronic defibrillators and pacemakers rather than competitive cardiac implants manufactured by other business entities. Medtronic concealed the defective nature of its defective defibrillators from potential recipients thereof and conspired with physicians and hospitals to scam recipients of

Medtronic defibrillators. By dumping defective defibrillator inventories into an unsuspecting market rather than scrap the defective inventory, Medtronic reaped billions in pre-tax profits. Health care providers (like Lakewood Hospital) have benefited by the lucrative mark-up on Medtronic defibrillators plus over $30,000.00 in medical services billing for implantation of each of the defective devices.

9.

Although Adams is not suing Medtronic under "product liability" theories of recovery of damages or for damages in connection with violation of the Federal Anti-kickback Statute or for massive ripoffs of Medicare and Medicaid, Medtonic has demonstrated a history of conspiring with both hospitals and physicians to rip off Medicare and Medicaid (see USDOJ investigation, findings and press release pertaining to Medtronic's spinal fusion kits). Medtronic further has a history of concealing adverse product information from recipients of its cardiac implants, from the FDA and

Medicare/Medicaid. Medtronic dumped defective

defibrillators containing batteries that were subject to

short-circuiting into an unsuspecting market for two

years (2003-2005) as cited by Federal Judge James

Rosenbaum. Judge Rosenbaum also cited Medtronic for

withholding said defective battery information from the

FDA in order to equip new defibrillator models with the

same type defective batteries (perjury). Senator Charles

Grassley charged Medtronic in October 2007 with

criminal false advertising by launching in January 2007

a 100 million dollars mass media advertising campaign

directed at potential recipients of implantable cardiac

devices long after Medtronic management knew that the

advertised cardiac devices were potentially defective

and perhaps fatal.

10.

Medtronic has thus far escaped criminal

indictments by paying a hundred and fifty million or so

to the USDOJ to call off investigations thereby

protecting complicit physicians and hospitals. Medtronic

has reaped billions in profits for defective inventories while paying out a few hundred million in USDOJ settlements and settlement of civil suits. Nevertheless, Adams had no standing to sue Medtronic due to Federal Preemption of product liability suits and lack of incriminating evidence to bring suits based upon criminal acts until the USDOJ on December 12, 2011 announced a settlement with Medtronic in connection with bribing physicians to the tune of $1,000.00 to $2,000.00 for every Medtronic defibrillator which they recommended and implanted. Hospital staff knowingly acted in furtherance of the conspiracy orchestrated by Medtronic by going along with the defrauding of heart patients needing an implanted defibrillator/pacemaker in order to to reap the tidy mark-up plus major billings for related medical services which in fact constitutes a criminal conspiracy.

11.

Said criminal conspiracies have been directly responsible for Adams being knowingly and intentionally subjected to sub-standard medical care, breach of trust, and breach of duties to render an acceptable level of medical care established by the medical profession and governing medical boards. Said conspiracies seriously interfered with the physician/ patient relationship by substituting fraud and bribery for physician integrity, trust and independent medical judgment. Adams has suffered both personal injuries and financial damages (see prayer for relief) in connection with said criminal fraud and criminal bribery reinforced by physicians' recommendations (based upon said criminal bribery) which Adams relied on to his detriment. But for said pattern of criminal behavior orchestrated by Medtronic and the participation of physicians and hospitals in the criminal conspiracies perpetrated by Medtronic, Adams would not have suffered pecuniary and personal injury damages (see prayer for relief).

PRAYER FOR RELIEF

Wherefore,   Adams   respectfully   prays   this

Honorable Court for judgment against Medtronic and Lakewood Hospital jointly and severally and for an award to Adams of actual financial damages in the amount of $73,000.00 (seventy-three thousand dollars ---- approximate dollar amount billed to Adams for defective defibrillator and implanting); and for an award to Adams of compensatory damages in an amount to be determined by the trier of facts to compensate Adams for anxiety and depression, mental terror, sleeplessness, loss of consortium, future medical expenses and cardiac damage.

In addition, because Medtronic management inflicted said damages knowingly, intentionally, recklessly, and without regard for human life thereby demonstrating a depraved mindset, Adams further prays this Honorable Court for an award of punitive damages to be paid to Adams by Medtronic in an amount reasonably proportional to Medtronic's net worth and in an amount sufficient to dissuade others similarly situated from like conduct.

In addition, Adams prays this Honorable Court for judgment against Lakewood Hospital in the amount of $31,000.00 (thirty-one thousand dollars) for future surgical explanting of his defective Medtronic defibrillator. Because Lakewood Hospital through its employees/agents knowingly acted in furtherance of the criminal conspiracy perpetuated by Medtronic as described herein, Adams further prays this Honorable Court for an award to Adams of punitive damages to be paid by Lakewood Hospital in an amount to be determined by the trier of facts to dissuade others similarly situated from like conduct.

Adams hereby requests a jury trial.

Respectfully submitted,

//Phillip J. Adams

3515 Colorado Avenue
Eldon, Missouri 65026
(573) 392-1938
philjulieadams@gmail.com

Three copies of the edited suit tailored for the

individual filing the suit should be mailed to the clerk of the State Court having jurisdiction and venue (the State Court where the individual filing suit resides) along with the filing fee specified by the court clerk's office. A self addressed 9" x 12" postage paid envelope should also be included for the clerk to mail a court stamped copy of the suit back to the individual who filed the suit.

Note: If the State Court where the suit is filed requires a "Civil Cover Sheet" then visit with the court clerk rather than mailing in the suit and the clerk will help the filing individual fill out the Civil Cover Sheet. It is actually pretty simple to fill out. Get summons forms from the court clerk and have the clerk sign the forms. Fill out and attach a summons to a copy of your complaint to be served upon each Defendant. Have the County Sheriff's office actually serve the Defendants.

Step three: When the case gets to the "discovery stage" (interrogatories, depositions, subpoenas, requests for documents, and requests for admissions), then hire an attorney on a contingency basis to handle discovery matters and the actual trial. Do not under any circumstances attempt to handle the trial yourself unless you are legally trained with some actual trial experience. Even then, it is not a good idea to represent yourself at trial because of jury and judge bias against non-lawyers representing themselves.

Jurisdiction and venue for the sample complaints definitely lie within the State courts because there is no diversity of citizenship that would confer diversity jurisdiction upon the federal courts since the person filing suit and his/her implanting physician and implanting hospital will be from the same state and Medtronic does business in all fifty states.

If Medtronic's attorneys attempt to remove on the basis of diversity of citizenship, they will be subject to severe sanctions because the sample complaints allege a cause of action against the implanting physicians and hospitals for which every state's tort laws provide a remedy.

Other books and screenplays by Don Alexander

Don has twelve books and two screenplays available for purchase at Amazon.com. Go to Amazon.com and click on the "books" search bar. In the books search bar enter the title you wish to review and add "by Don Alexander." The title will pop up fully displayed with a back cover synopsis (what the book is about). You can also read some selected text from the title selected. To purchase a book or screenplay, click on "add to cart" and then proceed to "checkout"
The titles are:

Flight From Death (novel)
Flight From Death (screenplay)
Sorrowland
The Chemistry of Health
Lucifer's Lie
The Case for Life
Out of Darkness
The Breath of Life
Without Excuse
Beneath Judicial Robes (screenplay)
In the Light
Creative Life Force
The Medtronic Murders
Legal Self-help – Save a Bundle